Expanded Edition

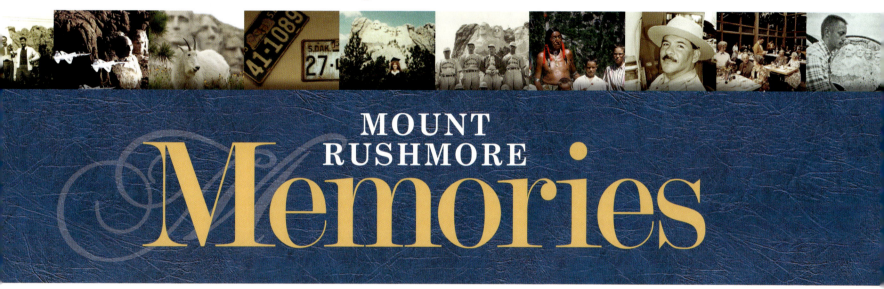

MOUNT RUSHMORE Memories

Association of Partners for Public Lands Media Award
Silver Independent Publisher Book Award

MOUNT RUSHMORE BOOKSTORES

Published by the Mount Rushmore Bookstores
Edited by Jean L.S. Patrick with Debbie Speas
Copy Editor: Mary Anne Maier
Designed by Amanda Summers Design
Project Manager: Debbie Speas
Printed in the U.S.A., using soy-based ink
ISBN-13: 978-0-9798823-5-7

©2011 by the Mount Rushmore Society
1st printing 2011; 2nd printing 2021
All rights reserved.
No part of this book may be used or reproduced without written permission of the publisher.

Mount Rushmore Bookstores
605-341-8883
mountrushmoresociety.com

As a committee of the Mount Rushmore Society, the mission of the Mount Rushmore Bookstores is to support and assist the National Park Service with educational, historical and interpretive activities at Mount Rushmore National Memorial.

Cover collage by Johnny Sundby Photography. Cover photos depict images of Mount Rushmore and the neighboring region throughout the years. Inside photos without credit were provided by the contributing author.

MOUNT RUSHMORE
Memories

Expanded Edition

Edited by Jean L.S. Patrick

with Debbie Speas

Published by the Mount Rushmore Bookstores

COLLECTING MEMORIES

The Mount Rushmore Memories project began in December 2010 when an appeal was sent across the nation, requesting people to submit a Mount Rushmore memory that encapsulated what Mount Rushmore meant to them. The response was overwhelming. Approximately 100 people offered their memories, including visitors, employees, local residents, National Park Service workers, Congressional representatives, longtime Rushmore supporters, a former Rushmore carver and the grandchildren of Doane Robinson, Charles Buell and Gutzon Borglum.

This expanded edition includes a few "new" memories, gathered in recent years, to add to the diversity of the Mount Rushmore story.

TIMES CHANGE

Please note that some activities described in this book, such as climbing the faces, hiking to the Hall of Records, taking helicopter tours, collecting rocks, etc., are no longer allowed at Mount Rushmore National Memorial. Many of the memories detailed in this book are just that . . . memories. Please inform yourself of all National Park Service regulations at www.nps.gov/moru before visiting the park.

SALLIE TAYLOR ZAMBELLI

Contents

Early Years *7*

Early Visitors *15*

Ben Black Elk *21*

Love & Family *25*

Presidential Views *33*

Visiting Faces *37*

Local Moments *43*

Laughter *49*

Rare Views *53*

Ceremonies and Celebrations *57*

Reflections *63*

Looking Ahead *71*

More to Remember *75*

Your Memory *79*

Introduction

Dear Reader:

The idea for this book was generated at a Mount Rushmore Society board of directors' retreat in which everyone was asked to explain what Mount Rushmore meant to him or her. While some spoke of our founding fathers and great artistic feats, most people told about personal experiences with family and friends at Mount Rushmore which generated lifelong, emotional connections to the park. Each memory was moving and gave deeper meaning to why people visit, volunteer, work or even get married at Mount Rushmore.

The same goes for me. Although I am inspired by the beauty of the mountain, by the ideals that four men left to a nation and by the fortitude of local men and women to raise money to keep this project on track, my most precious Mount Rushmore memory is the 2006 Independence Day Celebration & Fireworks event. This was the last day I spent with my dad, Tom Moses, before he became ill. Mount Rushmore was the backdrop for mixing patriotic music, energy and fireworks with moments of conversation with him. Since he passed away a couple months later, the picture taken that day is the last one I have of him—a picture that symbolizes sweet connection and a lasting smile.

July 3, 2006: A snapshot of a father and daughter's last memory together.

As I have found, a place has many purposes. As you share in the memories of this book, I encourage you to think about how your own Mount Rushmore memory has connected you to history, to art, to this country and to others.

Debbie (Moses) Speas, COO
Mount Rushmore Society
Rapid City, SD

The Needles in Custer State Park where Doane Robinson's idea for a carving in the Black Hills was born.
SHUTTERSTOCK

Early Years

An Idea Is Born

I remember my dad pointing out the spot where Gramp was standing when the idea for a carving came into his mind. According to the story, it was 1923 and they were going over the Needles Highway for the first time—my mother, my dad, his sister, my Gramp and a WWI friend of my dad's, Lester Atwood.

They were traveling in a Model T Ford touring sedan. The cooling system of this sedan was not what we have today, and they always carried a canvas bag on the front of it. When it got hot, they'd fill it with water and cool it off. Anyway, they'd run out of water, and my dad went down to the creek bed to fill the water pouch. When he got back up to the top, my Gramp was looking at the Needles, and off the cuff he started talking about his ideas and how it would be a great place for some carving.

I remember that Gramp was very sincere in everything he did. He was sincere about his feelings for his church, for his family, for his buddies and also for Mount Rushmore and South Dakota. He loved South Dakota.

When our family lived in Pierre, Gramp lived next door to us. The worst thing he ever said when he got irritated was "Oh, Thunder!" He played a lot of cards, but he never played on Sunday. He hated debt and attended church as regularly as possible.

Doane Robinson (standing) was the state historian of South Dakota and is credited for having the first idea for a carving in the Black Hills.

When I was between the ages of two and eight, my best friends were Pete and Karl Wegner. Their mother was Nellie Norbeck, Peter Norbeck's daughter. Peter Norbeck lived across the street, and Pete and Karl lived across the alley. We played together constantly. Little did we know that we had two unique grandfathers. We thought that everyone had grandfathers who did things!

Will Doane Robinson
Mount Rushmore Society Member
Rapid City, SD

Peter Norbeck served as senator from South Dakota from 1921 to 1936 and helped secure money from the U.S. government to carve Mount Rushmore. He also designed Iron Mountain Road and the tunnels that frame the sculpture. SOUTH DAKOTA STATE HISTORICAL SOCIETY

Looking for a Job

When Gutzon Borglum started carving Mount Rushmore in 1927, I was six years old and living in Keystone, South Dakota. The local residents were happy to have a new project begin that brought good jobs to the community. I knew many of the men who were hired to work at Rushmore because I delivered the *Rapid City Journal* to them.

In the mid-1930s when the Rushmore mail truck came to Keystone, I often put my bicycle in the back of the truck and rode up to Mount Rushmore, a three-mile trip. The cable car hoist operator would telephone Lincoln Borglum, the sculptor's son, to say, "Nick is here and wants to ride up to the top in the bucket." Lincoln always agreed to let me ride up with the next load of supplies. After spending a few hours watching the workers, I ran down the wooden stairway and coasted back to Keystone on my bicycle. I was looking for a job, but they did not hire anyone my age.

Lincoln Borglum was an avid baseball fan, and in 1938 he wanted Mount Rushmore to sponsor the Keystone baseball team. At that time I was 17 and working in the Etta Mine, running a jackhammer. Lincoln knew I was a good baseball player, and he hired me to work at Mount Rushmore so I could also play on the baseball team. The Keystone team became known as the Rushmore Memorial Drillers, and we went to the state tournament two years in a row.

I had a variety of jobs when I first started working at Rushmore. My brother, Charles, and I helped build the existing Sculptor's Studio. I earned 50 cents an hour. My first job on the carving was in the winch house on top of Washington's head where we raised and lowered the men who were drilling on the faces in the leather harness seats. I was paid 55 cents an hour.

That was a good job, but everyone wanted to be a driller because it paid more money. Eventually I drilled to the right of Lincoln's beard, but most of my drilling was below the chin of Roosevelt. As a driller, I earned 65 cents an hour. These were good wages during the Depression. We worked eight hours a day, six days a week.

Now, 70 years later, my best memory is having known Mr. Borglum and Lincoln Borglum and having had the opportunity to work on the famous carving. I also remember the other workers who helped carve the mountain. It is very rewarding for me to see visitors from all over the world come to admire this national monument.

Don "Nick" Clifford
Last living Mount Rushmore Worker
(1921–2019)

Pickup Memories

I was six years old when my daddy worked with Gutzon Borglum on the Mount Rushmore project. We lived in a little frame house in Keystone. One of my prize possessions is a picture of my father and me in a pickup truck, and in the back of the truck is a model of one of the presidential figurines.

Harold P. Munck
Mount Rushmore Archives

Harold's father served as "clerk of the works" for Gutzon Borglum. During the first months of the carving, he added an inspirational message to each page of the Daily Record.

Famous Fathers

My grandfather, Charles Buell, was an original booster of the Mount Rushmore project and served as fundraiser and ally.

On August 10, 1927, when a consecration ceremony was held at Rushmore Rock, Granddad shared the stage with President Coolidge who presented the first drill bits to sculptor Gutzon Borglum to begin the carving of the monument. Granddad's task that day was to justify to the audience gathered why George Washington should be memorialized in Harney Peak granite.

The Mount Rushmore Memorial team with Nick Clifford, pictured on the front row, far right.
NATIONAL PARK SERVICE

The *Rapid City Journal* reported, "Judge Charles J. Buell spoke of Washington, hero and leader, whose life presented an eloquent story of the possibilities of American citizenship, whose precepts inspire Americans in every difficult situation." Borglum, demonstrating the same tenacity as Washington, climbed the mountain to drill the first points of what would become the eyes, the nose and the mouth of the Washington portrait.

President Calvin Coolidge, speaks during the 1927 dedication of Mount Rushmore in which he committed federal funds to the project. C.J. Buell is on the platform.
LINCOLN BORGLUM COLLECTION

Seventy-five years later, I had the rare opportunity to meet Mary Ellis Borglum Vhay, Gutzon Borglum's daughter, who participated as a young girl in the 1927 ceremony alongside her father and my grandfather. Mel, as they called her, returned to South Dakota in 2002 as a special guest at the anniversary celebration of that historical event, and I waited all day to meet her.

When I saw Mel approaching the exhibit area where I stood, I said to her, "My grandfather gave a speech alongside your father at the 1927 program," and I pointed to their names and photos on display. She smiled, surrounded by her admirers, and said quietly to me as if we shared a secret, "Isn't it fun having famous fathers?"

As she was whisked off to the evening ceremonies in the Mount Rushmore Amphitheater, I wondered if we all might feel some of Mel's joy in the memory of our ancestors when we gaze on the famous faces of our founding fathers.

Rhonda Buell Schier
Education Specialist (2004-2010)
Mount Rushmore National Memorial

Promoting South Dakota

My paternal grandfather, Doane Robinson, lived next door to our family in Pierre in an apartment on Summit Avenue. At intervals, he would eat his main meal at our house, so all of the conversation centered on Rushmore during my growing up years.

A year before I was born, he had presented his idea at a convention in Huron of creating a number of sculptures as a promotion for tourism in South Dakota. He recommended the Needles in the Black Hills, but in time, they were determined to be unstable due to their constant erosion. After a number of false starts, Gutzon Borglum was employed. While my grandfather disagreed with Gutzon frequently (usually about money), he always had great admiration for his incredible genius as a sculptor.

I remember that the way to the 1927 dedication site for Mount Rushmore was impassable for automobiles. Pedestrians

President Calvin Coolidge, wearing a cowboy hat and boots, after offering Suzanne Robinson a ride on his horse, Mistletoe.
LINCOLN BORGLUM COLLECTION

and horses were the only means. As we were walking along, President Calvin Coolidge approached us, riding a horse. He stopped, kindly asking me if I would like to ride with him on his horse. I answered in the negative, explaining that my great aunt (Sadie or Sarah Ellen) wouldn't be able to ride. That concluded my amiable acquaintance with our president.

When the first of the "faces" was dedicated, Billy Doane Robinson (as my brother was called then) had the honor of being chosen to wave the flag, signifying the lifting of the flag covering Washington's face. I was jealous of him, as I was the oldest in our family, and said, "Boys always get to do everything."

I have a snapshot of Gramp, as we called him, under which he wrote, always the poet:

At 82, 'tis not so dreary as it would seem.
It's God's given time to dream.

It's as if he hadn't spent his entire life dreaming. Instead, he was diversified and worked unceasingly on a number of projects to promote South Dakota, Rushmore being only one of many. He continued this effort, hunting and pecking on his L.C. Smith typewriter to an advanced age prior to his death in November 1946.

Suzanne Robinson Dixon
Mount Rushmore Society Member
Sioux Falls, SD

Washington Dedication, July 4, 1930. RISE STUDIO

Laughter on the Mountain

When I visit Mount Rushmore, I always remember my late friend, Howdy Peterson. For 13 carving seasons (1929-1941), Howdy climbed to the mountain's top each morning as part of the crew that created the Memorial. Mostly he repaired equipment up there, starting at age 20.

By the time I got to know him, half a century later, he was seldom at a loss for a good Rushmore story. Many centered on sculptor Gutzon Borglum. Howdy recalled Borglum staring at the unfinished granite faces for hours, studying how the sunlight illuminated them as the day progressed. Finally, Howdy told me, Borglum would swing down from the tops of the heads "and with red paint he'd mark to take off three inches here, five inches there. It amazed me how he could do that."

Rushmore carvers, Howdy said, were all male and mostly young. Pranks were commonplace. Sometimes a man would go over the edge of the mountain in a swing seat and coworkers would pull his support cables back up, slowly so he wouldn't notice. "Then we'd let go and for about two feet he'd think he was falling off the mountain," Howdy laughed. Pretty funny, he assured me, if you worked up there and knew the guys.

I can still hear Howdy's laugh!

Paul Higbee
Spearfish, SD

Details, Details

My grandma worked as the executive secretary to the director of the park service in St. Louis while the mountain was being carved. When the Mount Rushmore crew needed more supplies—according to my grandma and her friend—they would send handwritten tickets to St. Louis to replenish the supplies.

She got one of these supply tickets requesting some additional winches, and so she typed it up to send to supply. Well, supply got the note, went to fill it and then came to talk with her. Apparently there was a problem

MOUNT RUSHMORE MEMORIES

Sarah's grandmother was Mary C. Waid Honeywell, who worked as executive secretary to John Nagle. A similar story about winches (shown above) and wenches was told by a secretary who worked under Gutzon Borglum. BELL PHOTO

with the spelling. They said that Mr. Borglum would probably want additional "winches," not additional "wenches."

Sarah Center
Mount Rushmore Archives

Growing Up Rushmore

Born in 1927 in the Black Hills, I grew up with Mount Rushmore. Along with my father, Edwald Hayes, I attended all of the major dedications or unveilings of each president's bust at Mount Rushmore, including George Washington in 1930, Thomas Jefferson in 1936, Abraham Lincoln in 1937 and Theodore Roosevelt in 1939. I also was present for the 1991 dedication which celebrated the completion of Mount Rushmore in 1941.

My father was the hoist engineer for about seven years. On several occasions over a number of summers, my mother would pack a lunch for me, and I would go to work with him and stay the full shift. He would hoist the first five men to the top of the mountain in the cable car. One of the men would ask, "Bobby, do you want to ride up with us?" Sure, they always had room for a little boy.

I would run around on the top of the mountain and visit with the winchmen, toolmen, powdermen and others. I knew all the men because most of them lived in Keystone, and I went to school with their kids. I would wave at the drillers who were drilling below. I would go back down and eat lunch with my father and the other men in the tool dressing shop.

During the afternoon I did physical work that contributed to the carving of Mount Rushmore. I unloaded the lunch buckets from the cable car and stacked them neatly near the hoist house. I also helped my father load and unload drill steel in and out of the tramway bucket. They processed from 300 to 500 pieces of drill steel each day.

I remember Borglum saying, "Hayes, you have a fine boy."

At the time I did not realize the importance of this project and what I was experiencing. This was just part of growing up. I guess I thought all boys had a similar playhouse.

Bob Hayes
Keystone, SD

A blacksmith sharpens drill bits during the carving of Mount Rushmore.
NATIONAL PARK SERVICE

Lighting the Faces

My father, Henry R. Scott, owned the Rapid Electric Company for 40 years (1927-1967), the company that eventually installed the lamp banks to illuminate Mount Rushmore for the very first time.

It was an exciting time for my family. Even though I was married and living in eastern South Dakota at the

Mount Rushmore illuminated at night. RODGER SLOTT

time, we spent summers with my parents and made many trips to watch the progress on the lighting project. My brother Albert (who now lives in Tucson, Arizona) worked on the project.

I also remember the summer after I graduated from high school. Four of my friends and I spent a week in a cabin near Keystone. One day we hiked up to Mount Rushmore and climbed the steps to the top. At that time, there were no restrictions. It is a great memory to have stood on the head of George Washington and to have seen the beginning of the Hall of Records, even if it was never completed.

My favorite vacation spot is still the Black Hills of South Dakota. This always includes a trip to Mount Rushmore to see the changes and wonderful improvements, to walk around the bottom of the mountain and to relive many happy memories.

Shirley Scott Cooper
Willmar, MN
Born August 23, 1924, in Rapid City, SD

Waiting for FDR

I remember an exciting day in 1936. It was when President Franklin D. Roosevelt came to visit Mount Rushmore! It was a Sunday, and he took a car from Rapid City to get here.

The *one* park ranger stationed at Mount Rushmore at the time came down to my cousin's shop in Keystone to direct traffic. My cousin was Josephine Hesnard who operated a mine-touring business where the Presidential Wax Museum is located now. The ranger directed traffic to park at this area until after the president had arrived. This was to ensure that there would be no dust from the gravel road while the president was traveling to the mountain since he was traveling in a shiny black convertible touring car.

BELL PHOTO

We waited and waited, not knowing that Guy March, who was one of the people meeting the president, had taken him to church.

The president finally arrived, and I remember him waving continually to everyone parked at my cousin's shop as he drove by ever so slowly in his open car.

Once up to the makeshift parking area at the base of mountain operations, he was greeted by a flyover. This was a tiny cub plane. Well-wishers had sent telegrams to the president through the Rapid City telegraph office. They were bundled up and dropped over the president's parking area—but not before a roll of bathroom tissue had been tossed out to determine the wind currents!

Though not planning a speech, Borglum urged the president to say a few words, which he did from his car due to the effects of polio. It was an inspiring event!

Geraldine (Hesnard) Evans
Mount Rushmore Society Member
Brighton, CO

The Tram

I remember going to Mount Rushmore as a kid. The minute my sister and brother and I got out of the car, we'd run up the stairs, all the way to the top.

One time, I got to ride in the cable car with my dad, my grandfather (Doane Robinson), my brother and Gutzon Borglum. It scared me to death, but I was going to go anyway. It was just a box for carrying the workmen up and down, but it was a thrill for me. I remember it was kind of jerky, and every time it jerked, my heart flip-flopped! I didn't look over the edge. Instead, I think I was looking up and praying that it wouldn't fall down.

We were there every summer and even lived in the Hills for a year. Mount Rushmore was part of our life.

Now, we take our families. In 2009, the Mount Rushmore staff named June 27 as Doane Robinson Day and treated us like royalty. Our children and their kids had the privilege of going on top. For them (and for all of us), it was a really big moment.

Barbara Robinson Nelson
Mount Rushmore
Society Member
Yankton, SD

The tram that Barbara Nelson rode with Gutzon Borglum and her grandfather, Doane Robinson. RISE STUDIO

A worker honeycombs the granite with a pneumatic drill.

LINCOLN BORGLUM COLLECTION

Early Visitors

Trunk Memories

In 1933, my dad, mother and two aunts decided to drive the 300 miles of graveled roads from Artesian, South Dakota, to Mount Rushmore. The auto was a 1932 Chevrolet coupe. The problem? In addition to the four adults, my cousin and I were also family members. Where could they put us girls? Problem solved! Dad tied open the trunk and fixed pillows amongst the suitcases so we could have a rear view of the Black Hills.

Our first view of Mount Rushmore was not the present-day profile of George Washington. Instead, we saw a profile of President Jefferson on the left of President Washington. What a surprise that poor-quality granite forced sculptor Borglum to blast away Thomas Jefferson and move him to the other side of George Washington.

Eleanore Rowan Moe
Rapid City, SD

As Jefferson appeared before his image was blasted off the mountain and moved to the other side of Washington.

Watching the Workers

My family made annual visits to Mount Rushmore in the 1930s. It was a big event to go to the log visitor center's porch or deck and watch the workmen who were in swing-like chairs and suspended by cables so they could carve the rock.

The time I remember was about 1937 or 1938, when I was about 12 years old. My family hiked and climbed to the top of Mount Rushmore.

There was a trail on the backside of the mountain that led to steps—a lot of steps that took you to the top. It was an effort! The view from the top was grand. Harney Peak stood out, of course.

What was most interesting to watch were the workers, men sitting in suspended seats using huge drills (like the ones used in the Homestake Mine in Lead), carving the faces. I think it was Jefferson's nose they were working on, maybe it was Washington's. But what amazed me was how the drills created "pockmarks" a few inches deep, so the face was not smooth when seen close up. It was quite a sight and looked like a hazardous occupation.

Doris Hehner
Rapid City, SD

Early Road Rage and Other Mischief

South Dakota became a state in 1889. Fifty years later in 1939, Mount Rushmore had a statehood celebration.

So Mom, Dad, my brother, his high school friend and I packed some snacks and took off for Mount Rushmore in the early afternoon. My dad, being a careful driver when going around all the curves, was shook up when a strange car came speeding out of nowhere onto the highway. It would have broadsided us except for the alertness of my father. My dad "blew a fuse" and was determined to follow the lone driver and tell him off!

Well, we lost him in the heavy traffic and went on our way with us kids giggling quietly in the back seat. I was 14, and my brother and his friend were 20. Parking was limited, so most people parked way below and rode in caravans in chosen cars to the viewing area. There were speeches over a loud speaker, including one given by the South Dakota governor.

At that age, I chose to hang on to my brother and his friend rather than stay with my folks. The boys decided to sneak up the "closed" wooden stairs that the workers used to get to the top of the monument. We came to a locked gate next to a cliff of rock, and the boys climbed over and pulled me over to the upper side. It was scary because it would have been bad for me if they had dropped me!

We climbed toward the top and snooped around the Hall of Records cut into the solid rock and then bravely walked over to the top of Washington's head and decided that would be a good spot to watch the fireworks!

What a beautiful clear night that was and how exciting to watch the fireworks. No one knew we were up there, and we were pretty proud of our naughty "accomplishment"! And then it was time to go back down. It didn't bother the fellows, but I was kind of scared! They had to pull me over that gate again. But all went well, and we made it back to our parents. I suppose we then bragged at what we did.

Next, we stood with a long line of people waiting for the vehicles that would take us back to our cars down below. My brother and his friend crawled in the back of a pickup. Dad, Mom and I were in the next car with a lone man. We could see my brother and friend pointing and laughing at us, but we didn't know why.

Dad had a great conversation with the driver from New York. When we got out of the car, they were still talking, and then he drove off to pick up more folks. The boys could hardly contain themselves when they pointed out to Dad that he was the man who almost hit us! Dad never spoke a word all the way home!

Janice (Humphryes) Baldwin
Born in Lead, SD
Graduated from Lead High School in 1943

Connections

I grew up climbing all over Mount Rushmore when we visited Mr. Borglum, who was a good friend of my mother. We were at Mount Rushmore a lot, and I have memories of being raised up the face of the monument in a canvas bosun chair to the top.

As an adult, I talked with the historian at Fort Robinson, Nebraska (where my mother and I lived in the 1930s and early 1940s), and asked if he had any information about Gutzon Borglum and how my mother would have gotten to know him so well.

The man at Fort Rob told me that Mr. Borglum was a great friend of the

The South Dakota statehood and the dedication of the Theodore Roosevelt figure were celebrated together on July 2, 1939. Twelve thousand people, including Janice Baldwin, were in attendance. NATIONAL PARK SERVICE

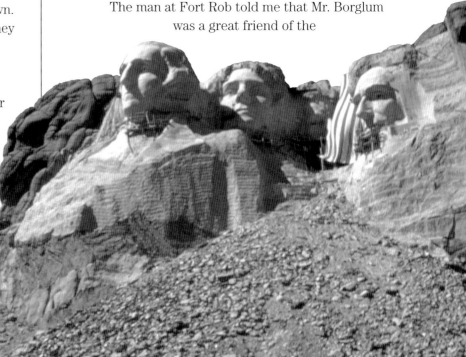

commandant of the post and came there often for hunting and fishing. This then made sense to me because my grandfather was the post engineer, and therefore in the same social strata as the commandant, so their paths would have crossed socially.

I hope to get to Mount Rushmore again.

Joann Gott Marra
Mount Rushmore Archives

Marra's mother was H. Betty Gott, a professional photographer.

A page from Becky's diary and the photo of Becky Terry on top of Washington's head.

National Parks or Bust!

In 1940, my parents, Myron and Mary Terry, my brother, Dick, and I drove from Ohio to Vancouver, British Columbia, in a General Motors "Carry All," headed for Shanghai, where my parents were missionaries. This was the furlough year, and our trip back to China was the sight-seeing trip of all time—every national park and monument they could get us to.

On July 25, 1940, we visited Mount Rushmore, which was under construction. My parents rode across in a cable car, but we kids climbed up and down (and did our legs ever ache!). On top, workmen were chiseling from baskets slung in front of the heads, but it was fairly quiet behind.

I had to do something spectacular to remember the occasion, so I climbed up on Washington's head and had my picture taken. Ever after that, when anyone mentioned Mount Rushmore, I was sure to point out that I had stood on Washington's head!

I faithfully kept a diary—which got waterlogged when our ship burned at sea in 1943. However, the good American 1940 ink made it through!

Becky Terry
Blaine, WA

Rushmore Honeymoon

We took photos of Mount Rushmore when we were on our honeymoon there on September 21, 1940. We stayed in a log cabin for 10 days at Silver City, a pretty valley with a railroad, road and creek nearby.

When we visited Mount Rushmore, we parked our car and walked up to the base. There was building equipment around but no workmen, so we walked up the wood plank stairs below Lincoln's visage. It was some climb! This was quite a nice stairway with plank railings. Then we came out on top of the Rushmore monument.

We walked along the plank walkway and saw workmen around using air guns on the rock. They waved to us and we went on to the top of George Washington's head. A workman was in a boxed-in sort of carriage, suspended along the side of Washington's head, drilling chunks of rock. He waved and grinned to us—we got his picture—and he handed us a piece of the chipped rock.

One of the pictures the Towerses took on their honeymoon.

Up on top of Washington's head, the rock sloped off in all directions—there were no railings or hand holds. Nobody told us to get out of there or waved us away. We were the only "civilians" on the rock.

After photographing the scenery, we went back down, looking in on a room-sized hole, the "museum,"* which was partially dug out of the solid rock behind the presidents' heads. It contained just building equipment and supplies.

Being on top of George Washington's head is really something to remember!

Jack and Rhoda Towers
Mount Rushmore Archives

*The "museum" referred to is the Hall of Records.

Trains and Automobiles

A couple of friends and I visited Mount Rushmore and the surrounding area in the spring of 1941. Two of us worked for the Chicago, Milwaukee, St. Paul and Pacific Railroad, so we took the train to Rapid City, South Dakota.

Since there were no bus tours at the time, we rented a cab from Rapid City for the day. There was snow in some sections of the Hills and on the road. The weather was mild, as we all wore sweaters or light jackets, including the two cab drivers. Needless to say, we enjoyed the trip very much.

Floryan Sabacinski
Mount Rushmore Archives

Sabacinski and friends pose for the camera.

B-17 Flyby

In 1943 or 1944, Edward J. Spevak, who served in the U.S. Air Force during World War II, flew from Florida to visit his family in rural Rupert, Idaho. He didn't land at Mount Rushmore. However, he did a flyby and took a photograph from his B-17.

Edward Spevak
Mount Rushmore Archives

Rushmore via Iron Mountain Road

My first visit to Mount Rushmore was as a high school student in the 1930s. My dad had a big maroon Dodge that we used to cruise around in. He loaded us all up—

my two sisters, my brother and me, and of course my mother—and the six of us headed to the Black Hills.

This was during the drought period when water was in short supply. (I remember going out there with our tongues hanging out!) Near Mount Rushmore, we found a wonderful spring. The Black Hills water was just great.

Then we started on that winding road* up to Mount Rushmore. I was watching every second of the way, and all of a sudden, there was George Washington's face in one of the tunnels. My father slowed long enough for us to have a look. Then we went through another tunnel where we saw another glimpse, all of which heightened our curiosity and anticipation. When we broke into the clear, we could see all of Mount Rushmore.

I think it was one of the most meaningful thrills of my life. I'd always loved history, especially American history, and there it was—right in front of me. George Washington, the father of our country. Thomas Jefferson, the author of the Declaration of Independence. Theodore Roosevelt, the "Rough Rider." And my favorite, Abraham Lincoln, with his brooding sad face. Gutzon Borglum had captured the mood and approach to life of all four of these great men.

I love Mount Rushmore. I don't think the day will ever come when I get tired of driving that winding road and ending up in front of those four majestic faces.

George McGovern
U.S. Senator from South Dakota (1963-1981)
Mitchell, SD

*The "winding road" that he refers to is Iron Mountain Road.

Picnicking

As a young girl, Florence Dion watched the face of George Washington come alive. She lived in Lead, South Dakota, between the years of 1926 and 1934 and remembers her family's trips to Mount Rushmore.

> … We always left early in the morning, and the drive to the mountain was slow. The roads were not paved and were very bumpy.

> … We always packed a picnic and ate while we watched the carving. My sisters and I loved the explosions.
>
> … My dad, Paul Dion, constantly read the paper and would explain the latest changes while we watched.
>
> … No one was allowed close to the mountain because the rocks flew a long way after each explosion. It was scary sometimes to watch some of the men swinging around when the explosions happened and the rocks flew.
>
> … My sisters and I wanted to run around in the woods, but after we got poison ivy once (or poison oak), our mother, Maude, didn't let us. Also, she didn't want us to get lost or get dirty.
>
> … I loved the smells around the mountain.

Florence Dion Buehring
Minneapolis, MN
As written by Andrea Cottrell of Minneapolis, MN

The powder men cut the sticks of dynamite and loaded them into holes that had been drilled into the mountain. At noon and at 4:00 p.m., the blasts were fired. These explosions carved the faces to within a couple of inches of the presidents' "skin."
BELL PHOTO

The Griffith brothers (Jim, Tom, Mike and Mark) pose with Ben Black Elk.

Ben Black Elk

Fifth Face on the Mountain

Ben Black Elk and his wife spent their summers in Keystone, South Dakota. He was also known as "the fifth face on the mountain" because he greeted visitors to Mount Rushmore and posed for pictures up at the mountain an estimated five million times from the 1950s through the 1970s. It was a pleasure to visit with him and listen to his stories. Those stories would be serious ones about the Lakota people and about his father (the famed Lakota holy man, Nicholas Black Elk) or funny comments that people would make to him about Mount Rushmore. He would always have a hearty laugh when sharing comical statements made by the tourists.

Bonita (Mohler Cochran) Ley
Mount Rushmore Society Member
Rapid City, SD

Equality

I have vivid memories as a youngster of talking to Ben Black Elk, a Native American, every time my parents took me to Mount Rushmore. Ben was a fixture at Mount Rushmore for many years. He was admired by tourists and probably had his picture taken as often as they took pictures of Mount Rushmore itself. His presence at the Shrine of Democracy reminded visitors that everyone is equal and that the original Americans are part of our national heritage.

James S. Nelson
Mount Rushmore Society President (1999-2005)
Rapid City, SD

A Cherished Memory with Siblings

To a small boy on a grand adventure with his grandfather, the four faces of Mount Rushmore National Memorial were not only larger than life—they were as big as the world could get. But, in the shadows of the massive mountain memorial, surrounded by sweet-smelling ponderosa pines and scurrying chipmunks, I saw a "fifth face."

His skin, seemingly weathered to a dark brown parchment by decades of ceaseless sun and wind and rain, would remain seared in my memory long after the four faces of freedom had faded in the rearview mirror of my grandpa's car. His quiet nature, so unlike the cacophony of sound and shrieks from my siblings and cousins, was so welcomed, and now, decades later, so fondly recalled.

I never knew how many years Ben Black Elk stood below America's Shrine of Democracy, proudly posing for pictures with visitors from around the world. Certainly, he still stands silently in a million fading photo albums recounting family vacations to our nation's heartland.

I only know that in my mind's eye, and in my most cherished childhood memories, he stands there still.

Thomas D. Griffith
Mount Rushmore Society Member
Deadwood, SD

Black Elk Speaks

As a 16-year-old visitor to Mount Rushmore in 1965, I did not realize that having my picture taken with "the fifth face of Mount Rushmore" and some young relatives would become part of a lesson in my high school classroom more than two decades later. Of course, this "fifth face" was

A Friendship Language

It was at Mount Rushmore when I first learned my father spoke fluent Lakota. His father's homestead bordered the Rosebud Reservation, and he'd picked it up from playmates. The first time we heard him in conversation with Ben Black Elk, we were awestruck.

Their relationship lasted many years as they went to travel shows across the country to promote the monument, the Black Hills and South Dakota. One of their favorite ploys was to start telling jokes in Lakota and to laugh uproariously, thus drawing a crowd to their booth.

Eileen Fleishacker
Mount Rushmore Society Member
Rapid City, SD

The "fifth face of Mount Rushmore" poses with Robert Roth (far right) and some relatives at the Shrine of Democracy in June of 1965.

Ben Black Elk, an Oglala Sioux, who greeted visitors to the Shrine of Democracy for many years.

Fast forward to the mid-1980s when I was preparing to teach *Black Elk Speaks: Being the Life Story of a Holy Man of the Oglala Sioux* in my Literature of the American West class at Laramie (WY) High School. I discovered that Ben was the son of Black Elk, featured in the popular book. I was floored by this revelation and felt a special connection to *Black Elk Speaks*. Later, I enlarged that picture taken so long ago to connect my students with the lesson.

Robert Roth
Laramie, WY

Tanyan yahe pelo.
Mount Rushmore National
Memorial. Ho wan oya
chikan inazin yon a oblotun
A Living Memorial epathan.

Words from the Lakota version of the Mount Rushmore Audio Tour, welcoming visitors to the Memorial and recognizing how the sculpture gazes out toward the Black Hills and releases emotions in all of us.

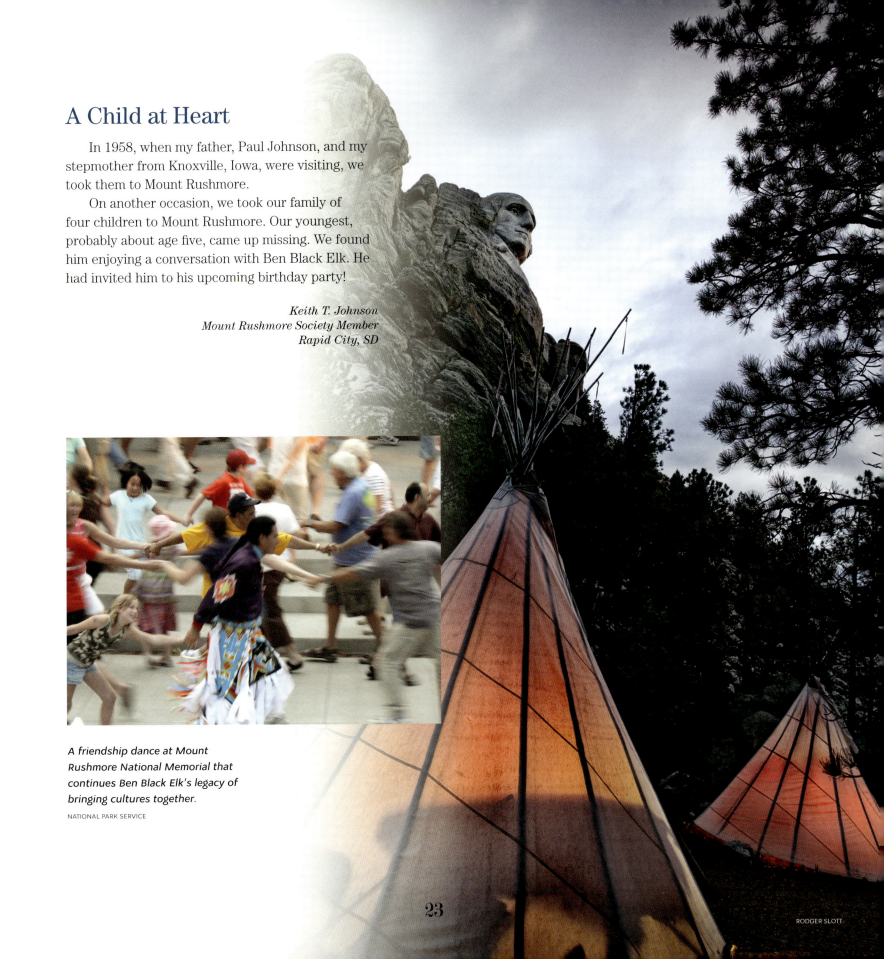

A Child at Heart

In 1958, when my father, Paul Johnson, and my stepmother from Knoxville, Iowa, were visiting, we took them to Mount Rushmore.

On another occasion, we took our family of four children to Mount Rushmore. Our youngest, probably about age five, came up missing. We found him enjoying a conversation with Ben Black Elk. He had invited him to his upcoming birthday party!

Keith T. Johnson
Mount Rushmore Society Member
Rapid City, SD

A friendship dance at Mount Rushmore National Memorial that continues Ben Black Elk's legacy of bringing cultures together.

NATIONAL PARK SERVICE

Full Circle: Nan Roberts and her mom on their last shared adventure.

Love & Family

Station Wagon Will Travel

I remember as a child going to Mount Rushmore and riding up the winding roads from the farm south of Hot Springs, South Dakota. Our family was driving in a big green station wagon that also was used for a school bus. My dad and my mom and sisters and I were having a fabulous time, and it was the best day of our lives. On the way home, we ran out of gas in Wind Cave Park, and of course someone stopped to help us in the 1960s. I wish I could go on that trip again.

Mary Kaplan
Mt. Juliet, TN

First Days

My husband and I went to Mount Rushmore following our wedding reception on June 5, 1965. We were going to be in Vermillion for the summer and then move to Chicago in August. We both had strong feelings for Mount Rushmore and knew it would be a year before we would be able to visit Mount Rushmore again.

When I am up at Mount Rushmore, I often reflect on our lovely memory of visiting Mount Rushmore on our wedding day.

Karen Raben
Mount Rushmore Society Member
Rapid City, SD

Full Circle

It's 1957, and there we are: Mom, Dad, my sister Bobbie, me, Ben Black Elk and Mount Rushmore.

I was three years old at the time. This was the start of our yearly family camping adventures. During almost two decades that followed, we literally "saw the USA in our Chevrolet." Of all the states we crossed and the sights we saw, the visit to Mount Rushmore would remain with me.

In April 2004, I lost my beloved father. Though widowed and 89 years old, my mother had not lost her love and enthusiasm for travel. In August 2004, 47 years after our first trip, I returned with her to Mount Rushmore.

Most of the visitors around us had no idea that the Avenue of Flags where we stopped was once where Ben Black Elk (son of the famous Oglala Lakota Holy Man, Black Elk) greeted tourists, shared history, posed for pictures and caused this tiny little girl to cling tightly to her mother's pant leg. It is possible that at this exact place and time, my love and reverence for the Native American culture began. How honored I am to have seen him and to remember him so vividly.

As Mom and I walked the old paths, climbed the same steps and paused at former viewing spots, the memories flooded back. If we closed our eyes, it was 1957 once more.

But on this trip in August 2004, we attended the Evening Lighting Ceremony for the first time. Arm in arm, Mom and I "ooo-ed and ah-ed," thrilled with the spectacle, thrilled to be there together.

On a cold winter evening in January 2005, I set up a small screen in my mother's bedroom and threaded the 1957 family vacation film through the old projector. There again was my father, in his early 40s, taking us back to Mount Rushmore, the Black Hills and a time long gone, but never ever forgotten.

My mother died two days later.

The significance of that last trip with my mother is greater than words can express. Who knew this would be her final trip, the last shared adventure?

The following year, with love in my heart and tears in my eyes, my husband and I returned to Mount Rushmore, where in a secluded spot visited decades before, we released into the wind a dusting of ashes and memories. Mount Rushmore has always been with me. Now, through my parents, I am a part of Mount Rushmore.

Nan Roberts
Middleton, WI
In loving memory of Willard and Viola Roberts

The License Plate Game

When I was a young single mother, entertainment didn't have much place in our budget. Living in Rapid City, we went to Mount Rushmore often to stroll through the parking lot to check out the license plates. I kept score, and we followed this ritual with a fast food dinner back in Rapid, with the winner picking the restaurant.

These days, when the kids (who are now in their 30s) visit the monument, they still shout, "Missouri!" "Arizona!" "Kansas!" and are not above giving each other a little shove, much to the chagrin of their children.

Eileen Fleishacker
Mount Rushmore Society Member
Rapid City, SD

Unchanging

I visited Mount Rushmore many years ago with my family, and I wanted my son to have the same experience I did. It has changed a lot since I was there about 35 or 40 years ago, but the view and the story are still the same.

Janet R. Earls
Fort Dodge, IA

Visits that Shape a Life

My first recollection of the Memorial came in March 1966 when I, a young Air Force lieutenant from Pennsylvania (who had never been west of the Mississippi), made the scenic drive from Ellsworth Air Force Base to see my childhood dream.

As I drove up the hill from Keystone, the first glimpse of the four faces took my breath away. I'll never forget walking up the winding pathway lined by state flags to the Buffalo Room, where I walked in the very footsteps of Eva Marie Saint and Cary Grant when they filmed the gripping shooting scene in *North by Northwest*. And the view from a window-side table as I enjoyed my first-ever bison burger was magnificent!

XANTERRA ARCHIVES

The mystique of the place brought me back several times that summer and continued into the fall when I met a local girl who later would become my wife. That winter we drove into the Hills several times with her three younger sisters and played in the snow in the shadow of the presidents.

After we were married and settled into an apartment in downtown Rapid City, a drive through the Black Hills ending at Mount Rushmore was always on the itinerary whenever family and friends came to visit. And later, when the service took us to California and a job brought us back east to live, we became the visitors.

Now I am at a point in life where physical limitations have made a trip back to Rapid City unlikely. But I have seen a true wonder of the modern world, and it has become an important part of my history and that of my family.

Ron Hasek
Pittsburgh, PA

First Kiss

In 1980, I was working as a seasonal park ranger at Jewel Cave National Monument and went on a date with one of my coworkers, another seasonal park ranger. Bill took me out to dinner at the Powder House Lodge in Keystone one warm summer evening, and following a fine dinner, we went to Mount Rushmore to see the sculpture lighting.

We walked to the viewpoint with the sculpture illuminated in the background, and Bill kissed me. That was our first kiss, and we were married in Yellowstone National Park in 1982. Fast forward to 2010: We returned to the Black Hills to live due to my new job as Mount Rushmore National Memorial's superintendent. We have come full circle.

Cheryl Schreier
Superintendent (2010–2019)
Mount Rushmore National Memorial
Mount Rushmore Society Member

Married on the Faces

I was eating breakfast with Gerard Baker, who was superintendent at the time, when I made the request. "Gerard," I said, "Diane and I are going to get married. Would you allow us to be married on the terrace?"

"Why would you want to get married on the terrace?" asked Gerard.

I explained that it was a great setting with a great backdrop, and I needed him to open the gates early so that our small party could be there before the tourists came.

Again Gerard asked, "Why would you want to get married there?" Again, I mentioned the scene and the setting.

"But why do you want to get married down there?" asked Gerard. "Why not get married up on the top?"

So on an August morning in 2007, my wife and I were married at the top of Mount Rushmore. It was a dual ceremony. Bruce Adams from the Methodist church in Deadwood led one part of the ceremony. Gerard, dressed in ceremonial garb, led the Native American portion. As we kneeled on a buffalo robe, Gerard sang and gave us the blessing of his people. It's a memory that I'm sure no one else has.

There's more to the story. Diane's son didn't make it to the wedding because he was stuck in an airport in Minneapolis. So his sister held up her phone so he could hear. It turns out that the reception is quite good on top of Mount Rushmore!

Sid Goss
Mount Rushmore Society Member
Deadwood, SD

A Dream

My mom, brother and I visited Mount Rushmore for the first time in June 2009, traveling all the way from Massachusetts. It was a moving and inspirational experience. It was a particularly memorable experience for me because we were able to take my mom there, wheelchair and all. She grew up during the Great Depression, so it was a blessing that we had the time and resources to be able to take her.

One last comment: I had been yearning to see Mount Rushmore ever since seeing the film *North by Northwest* with Cary Grant!

Jim Panagas
North Reading, MA

Helicopter View

My favorite memory of visiting Mount Rushmore was when my two sisters and I boarded a bubble-front helicopter to see the faces. The attendant took a picture of the three of us inside the helicopter. Then we flew up the mountain. What a thrill it was to see Mount Rushmore up close!

Dennis Daugaard
Governor of South Dakota (2011–2019)
Pierre, SD

Joyce, Sandy and Dennis Daugaard get a closer view of the faces.

Family Vacations

My family's first visit to Mount Rushmore was when my parents traveled the gravel road on their honeymoon in August of 1948. Mother was a bit afraid of the winding road up to the site. They were on their way to California to visit relatives but were touring the Black Hills first.

A few years later, in 1957, they took their three oldest children to the Black Hills to visit cousins in Lead, South Dakota. (I was one of these children.) We stopped to view Mount Rushmore. It was so amazing to see the four gigantic and grand faces of the presidents. We were allowed to spend a quarter to look closer at the faces through the telescopes. Dad shared that Mom's enjoyment was taking us to the souvenir shop. We each selected an item, like a super-long, round and fat pencil or a small cup and saucer or a billfold with Mount Rushmore written on it.

During the middle 1980s, I was married and had two children of my own. My husband and I took them to learn about Mount Rushmore. We walked up the long, gradual steps through the Avenue of Flags. Our boys were much quicker with the climb up to see the faces than we were. They were excited to view the four faces and were interested in the story told by the movie clips and pictures of the construction of this national monument.

As a second-grade teacher, I have found that students are so proud to raise their hands to show that they also have taken a family trip to see Mount Rushmore. In their wild imaginations, they would like to take a field trip to visit Mount Rushmore again!

Sandy Entringer
Corsica, SD

Now You See It, Now You Don't

I lived in Custer, South Dakota, from 2007 to 2009 and was able to visit Mount Rushmore many times. I was always amazed at how the monument was carved. But my favorite memory was with my parents when they visited in late May.

NATIONAL PARK SERVICE

They were in their mid-60s but had yet to see Mount Rushmore. I was soooo excited to share their first view of it.

But, alas, on the day we went, there was a huge fog bank covering the monument. It was quite funny, actually, once I got over the initial letdown. We stayed for a while, as the monument played "hide and seek" behind the fog. Occasionally different aspects would come into view. Luckily, my parents were able to see Mount Rushmore in all its glory later in the week.

Malee Prete
Bourne, MA

Lasting Legacy

It seems that every year we have one couple that has met at Rushmore and gets married; I am no exception. I can remember the day that I met my wife, Carol, and wouldn't trade that experience for anything in the world.

She started working at the Mountain Company in 1974, but my job as human resource director didn't leave much time for me to think about much besides my job. The next year, she started work in mid-April. Since it was so early in the season, the only other people around were Kay and Jack Riordan and several department supervisors. This allowed me to get to know her better.

The relationship grew, and we ended up getting engaged with plans to marry in September 1976. But after she was hired by the Hill City School District to teach kindergarten in January 1976, we decided to move the wedding up to May and then up to December. Boy, did the date changes start the tongues wagging among the employees. But we showed them—our first son wasn't born until 1980. (I think they had even started a betting pool!)

Russ Jobman
General Manager (1993–2014)
Xanterra Parks & Resorts
Mount Rushmore National Memorial

A Sucker for a Dare Devil

I worked as a summertime hostess at Powder House Lodge in Keystone, South Dakota, in the early 1960s. Powder House had waitresses, and the Buffalo Dining Room at Mount Rushmore had singing waiters. Needless to say, we girls were very excited when we went there to hear them sing and when they came to the Powder House for lunch! I will never forget one performance held in the amphitheater in which they sang a compilation of famous Western tunes. I've been singing "The Wells Fargo Wagon Is A-Comin'" for 50 years since.

I didn't wind up marrying a singing waiter, though. John Sundby, a helicopter pilot, courted me by hovering above the trees in full sight of the Powder House dinner guests and giving me a few rides over Washington's head. I am now Kathy Wittnebel Sundby.

Kathy Wittnebel Sundby
Rapid City, SD

A picture of some of the singing waiters who didn't get the girl!
XANTERRA ARCHIVES

A Lasting Love Affair

I saw Mount Rushmore for the first time in the 1940s on a family trip from my home state of Iowa. Although that trip was special, it was the time I spent working at Mount Rushmore for the Mountain Company in the late 1950s that is forever engrained in my heart and mind.

I remember well the beautiful, new employee dormitory built in 1956. At that time, the concession was

Visitors enjoy ice cream and souvenirs in the concessions building operated out of what was once known as Gutzon Borglum's Sculptor's Studio.
NATIONAL PARK SERVICE

in the Sculptor's Studio, which was a log building located on the present-day Borglum View Terrace. I remember working there at the soda fountain, which had a great view of the mountain.

The next year, 1957, I enjoyed working in the new concessions building (located where the Grand View Terrace is today) selling purses and small stuffed alligators in the leather department! A third summer I worked in the beautiful dining room, again creating wonderful memories with all my college friends— and older staff, too.

In the evenings, groups of us would play games and listen to records in the lower level of the dorm or hike around the area, where we'd sit on rocks and tell ghost stories or funny tourist stories. In August, we had fun joining the workers at the State Game Lodge for a great variety show in the park's old amphitheater. Summers always ended with a formal farewell party at the Alex Johnson Hotel, hosted by Kay and Carl Burgess.

Working summers at Mount Rushmore was a great opportunity to meet people from faraway places, explore the Black Hills and have some summer romances. But the greatest love affair of all was with the Memorial itself— one that I have had ever since.

Carolyn "Kitty" Claussen Mollers
Mount Rushmore Society President (1987-1993)
Chair of the Mount Rushmore Preservation Fund
($57 million was raised for park improvements in the 1990s.)
Rapid City, SD

In Memory of Ranger Darrell Martin 1965–2007

Assistant Chief of Interpretation at Mount Rushmore, American Indian Liaison Midwest Region NPS

During the spring and early summer of 2006, my husband, Darrell, had been very busy as he worked with his staff to plan events and programs for visitors to Mount Rushmore. In addition to all of this, he had to be away for training during the two weeks right before the Independence Day activities and fireworks on July 3rd.

That day was also our anniversary. While speeding out the door that morning, he told me that he'd try to have a lunch break with me "somewhere in the Amphitheater." Around 1:30 p.m., he did take a few minutes to quickly eat something, but away he went at a rapid pace once again. I had hoped for some time together, but I could see that this was not going to be the case at all.

That evening, in the middle of the ceremony, Superintendent Gerard Baker said that he wanted to spend a few minutes to give praise and thanks to his staff "for the effort and time they had put into preparing for the event, let alone working it." He pointed out Darrell and explained what his schedule had been like, and he finished with, "He has been so busy that he hasn't even had time to get to a store or go anywhere but the park. He asked me to say to his wife, 'Thank you for understanding and happy anniversary!'"

I remember thinking that I was very privileged to be in a spectacularly scenic place, celebrating a national holiday and a personal one with such dedicated people, especially my husband.

Darrell really loved the Mount Rushmore staff and always appreciated their commitment to the park service. Many of the people that he worked with are still here, and they have all been incredibly good to me. When I hear the words "Mount Rushmore," it is not the carved faces that I first envision. Instead, I think of the faces of those who work every day to make and keep the Memorial an inviting place: those folks who wear the green and gray.

Darrell was one of those.

Zane Martin
Curator
Mount Rushmore National Memorial

RAPID CITY JOURNAL

Mount Rushmore National Memorial
CHAD COPPESS

Presidential Views

The Birth of the Presidential Trail

During the redesign of the visitor services facilities, I was asked to design the Presidential Trail. I was fairly new to the design team at that time. The superintendent at that time, Dan Wenk, pointed up to the mountain and said, "Pat, why don't you go up there and tell us where to put a trail." I thought, "Well, okay, this sounds like fun."

For part of that summer, I hiked around the talus slope, looked over the Borglum haul routes and arrived at a plan for the Presidential Trail. I have to say that it was one of the more interesting projects I have been honored to design.

The Presidential Trail today.
SOUTH DAKOTA TOURISM

Patrick H. Wyss
Rapid City, SD

Lincoln Comes to Life

I have only been able to visit Mount Rushmore once in person. (All the films never did do it justice!) Most wonderful was the actor portrayal of President Lincoln. Mr. Lincoln has always been one of my favorite presidents. The actor was a wonderful inspiration and was very kind as well as friendly. He was so willing to share his knowledge and time with me. I do not remember his name, but I will remember him and how he made me feel. God bless him. . . . I hope to be able to come back soon.

Sandra Purcell

Dark Becomes Light

As a boy, probably ten or eleven years old, I accompanied my parents to an evening lighting in the 1950s. I recall racing along the paths, identifying different state flags and climbing each and every outcropping of granite in sight as we moved through the dark trees on the way to the visitor center and observation deck. Although the faces were impressive, chasing chipmunks was also exciting for me as we waited for the program.

There were limited lights, so when darkness arrived it was nearly black on the viewing terrace. You could hardly see the other visitors and certainly not the presidents on the mountain. Then it happened. While the National Anthem played, the huge lights exposed the white granite and the presidents literally jumped out of the darkness. Chills ran up and down my back. I was thrilled and awed by this experience.

This memory is still vivid for me. Every time I visit a Mount Rushmore Evening Lighting Ceremony, I experience this rush when the presidents appear out of the dark.

Tim Raben
Mount Rushmore Society Member
Rapid City, SD

MOUNT RUSHMORE MEMORIES

Sculpting the Presidents

As the sculptor in residence at Mount Rushmore during the 2001 and 2003 seasons, I enjoyed explaining how Gutzon and Lincoln Borglum created the bronze sculptures that are displayed throughout the Memorial. I also enjoyed learning so much about each of the presidents.

Peggy Detmers
Hill City, SD

Sculptor-in-residence Peggy Detmers during her employment at Mount Rushmore.

Magical View

The first time I ever saw Mount Rushmore was in 1986. I stepped out on the platform. They were playing the National Anthem, and I saw the faces. It was so awesome. I remember the goose bumps and tears.

Three years ago, we took our grandchildren to Mount Rushmore over spring break. It was April, and it was so foggy. We hung out and waited, cameras ready. Then we saw a most awesome sight: the fog lifted one face at a time. We were so awestruck that we forgot to take pictures.

Ralph and Marvella Walters
Bennington, NE

A View for the People

It was either the end of 1995 or the beginning of 1996 when the government shut down because of budget arguments. Nonessential government workers were put on furlough, and Mount Rushmore was closed.

During this time, a songwriter from New York and I headed to the Black Hills to write songs. It was winter, and I wanted Bill to see Mount Rushmore in the snow. The ropes were pulled across the old walkway and the old tiered parking lot wasn't plowed.

When Bill and I saw the rope across our path, I stamped my entitled little foot and said something like, "This is MY mountain, this is OUR monument, and they can't keep us from looking at it!" Bill may not have felt the ownership I felt as a South Dakotan, but he was always up for civil disobedience.

So we stepped over the rope and made our way toward the old viewing area. It was incredibly quiet, and it was snowing. We stood at a lesser-used viewing point and took it all in: the sound of the wind . . . the snow . . . the pine trees. No one else was there, and it was so peaceful.

Debra Weitala
Mitchell, SD

Those Guys on the Mountain . . .

Chipmunks, chipmunks, chipmunks. That was my first Mount Rushmore memory. As a young child (many years ago), the little critters were everywhere as we walked up the dirt path to the terrace area. And, there was such a wise and kind Ben Black Elk, who always

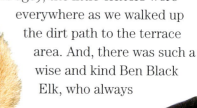

RODGER SLOTT

took the time to visit with us kids. And (oh yes), there were also those guys on the mountain.

Fast forward to memories from more recent times . . .

The beauty of snow falling over the mountain faces. The awesome Independence Day Celebration, with the boom of the jet flyover preceding the boom of the pyrotechnics. The tears of joy from our new citizens at the Naturalization Ceremony in the Amphitheater.

And finally, the feeling of pride in being an American every time I round the bend in the highway and see those guys on the mountain.

Ruth Samuelsen
Mount Rushmore Society Member
Rapid City, SD

The Avenue of Flags was redesigned for accessibility needs in 2020. The original columns displaying the flags were removed and the pathway expanded to better accommodate visitors as they make their way to the Grand View Terrace. The Society provides for the annual replacement of each flag on the Avenue of Flags, representing 50 states, one district, three territories and two commonwealths.

DEBBIE SPEAS

Visiting Faces

Cornerstone of South Dakota Tourism

My first visit to Mount Rushmore took place during my first family vacation in 1959. As an 11-year-old girl, I was impressed by the majesty of Mount Rushmore, but even more impressed by how much attention it got from the throngs of tourists who came from all over the country and the world.

I continue to be impressed by this attention as I proceed through my career as a historian. In the process of researching and writing about Black Hills tourism development, I have given a number of presentations at scholarly conferences in the United States and in Canada.

At one conference, a group of Australian scholars asked question after question about Mount Rushmore until we had to vacate the conference room to allow the next session to begin. At another conference, German participants quizzed me about Mount Rushmore during coffee breaks and lunches. United States scholars also have expressed deep interest in Mount Rushmore. Again, nearly everyone is surprised (and some of them are dubious) when they hear that the monument was not initiated as a federal undertaking, but by promoters from South Dakota.

What is most significant about Mount Rushmore to me is this ability to capture the attention and stimulate the curiosity of so many people. Mount Rushmore has brought millions of people to South Dakota, has helped to form the state's identity and has served as a cornerstone of its flourishing tourism industry.

Suzanne Julin
Missoula, MT

First Time, Every Time

About 15 years ago, I had the opportunity to travel to Sioux Falls on business. I had always been intrigued with Mount Rushmore and figured since I would be "so close," I would stay a few extra days, bring my then eight-year-old son with me and absorb a little good old American culture.

I have visited the beautiful Black Hills many times since then, and on each trip I visit Mount Rushmore at least once, usually twice. I love to see the monument in different lights, at different times of day and in different weather conditions. One of my memorable visits was in early October, first thing in the morning, when I was the only visitor. It felt so special to me.

But I will always remember the first time with my son like it was yesterday. We stood on the viewing deck, and I was speechless for several minutes. Finally Jack said, "You really like this, don't you, Mom?"

Linda Gallalee
Chicago, IL

A Television First

We visited there innumerable times over the years. On July 23, 1962, I was present during the first transatlantic television satellite broadcast via Telstar which was produced and sent from Mount Rushmore! The Mormon Tabernacle Choir sang "God Bless America" and other selections. It was exciting to be there for such an historic event.

Suzanne Robinson Dixon
Mount Rushmore Society Member
Sioux Falls, SD

MOUNT RUSHMORE MEMORIES

Piece of Art

All my life, I dreamed of visiting Mount Rushmore. On Saturday, Oct. 11, 2008, at 44 years of age, my dream came true.

The day was cloudy and rainy, and yet my favorite "piece of art" was still a spectacular site to behold. The God-given talent of the men and women who worked tirelessly to bring this national monument to life was truly amazing. I will never forget that day.

Lolita Maria Jones
Fort Washington, MD

Observations

Although I don't live in the Black Hills, I have the opportunity to visit Mount Rushmore often throughout the year. My favorite thing to do is to grab a giant chocolate ice cream cone, stroll up the Avenue of Flags (finding South Dakota's flag along the way) and sit on the Grand View Terrace to watch the tourists and listen to their reaction to the monument.

I love listening to the different accents and the many different stories about the presidents and the monument: some true, some a bit skewed and some just plain bunk! It's interesting to listen not just to their words, but to their tone as

The scale model that Gutzon Borglum used to create his piece of art. NATIONAL PARK SERVICE

RODGER SLOTT

well—just above a whisper, like they are in church. That awe and wonder strikes me every single time I am on the terrace.

Dawn Miller
Summerset, SD

Home Run!

I had the opportunity to meet former Minnesota Twins first baseman Kent Hrbek at a Governor Rounds Pheasant Hunt years ago. He had a 14-year career with the Twins and helped them win two World Series championships in 1987 and 1991. As fortune would have it, I then had the opportunity to hike to the top of Mount Rushmore with Herbie (that's what his friends call him!) and his family on a beautiful Black Hills day. He told me later that he used a photo of himself sitting on George's head as his screen saver! Unfortunately, I'm not in the picture.

Mike Derby
Mount Rushmore
Society Member
Rapid City, SD

The Black Hills Pull

I became a professional actress with the Black Hills Passion Play in 1986. The show was performed in Lake Wales, Florida, during the winter months, and I'll never forget when longtime cast members spoke of the beauty of the Black Hills and in particular of their landmark, Mount Rushmore. I knew little of the state and had only heard mention of the Black Hills, but I knew about Mount Rushmore.

When I first saw the monument on Memorial Day weekend in 1986, I was overwhelmed with a deep feeling of patriotism. The magnificent carving framed with 50 state flags left me speechless and reflective.

Now, when friends and relatives come to the Black Hills and when I greet guests at the Spearfish Chamber of Commerce Visitor Center, I encourage them to visit this most impressive, educational and awe-inspiring national monument.

Lisa Langer
Prior Executive Director
Spearfish Chamber of Commerce
Mount Rushmore Society Member
Spearfish, SD

Horses

My first memory of Mount Rushmore was when I visited the Black Hills with my family as a little girl. We would drive from Hamlin County to the Hills during the summer with our horses. There were some great trails we could ride that took us very close to the backside of the monument.

While I was growing up, my family wasn't very political, but still I knew, even as a little girl, that Mount Rushmore was important. It was awe-inspiring, and I was proud that it was in my home state.

Kristi Noem
Governor of South Dakota
Pierre, SD

Dignitaries

I have many, many memories of interesting events, people and challenges during my 19 years as chief park ranger at Mount Rushmore National Memorial. While working at the Memorial, I had the opportunity to meet and talk with, at least for a short while, three sitting U.S. presidents and five former heads of state from other nations. Two conversations stand out.

Israeli Prime Minister Ehud Barak visited within the year after the attacks on our nation on September 11, 2001, and talked with then Chief of Interpretation Jim Popovich and me about his thoughts of the need for the U.S. to take a very firm stance against terrorism (this coming from someone who had been in the heat of battle against terrorists during his life). When Popovich asked Barak if he would like to experience the visitor center exhibit simulating a dynamite blast during the carving of Mount Rushmore, Barak replied with something similar to "No thanks, I've seen enough of the real thing."

President Bill Clinton visited Mount Rushmore in July 1999. The president spent over an hour walking around the visitor center and Grand View Terrace, shaking hands with and talking to park visitors. Superintendent Dan Wenk was leading the group, and I was tagging along behind with some of the security detail.

The lights were now on the mountain sculpture. It was getting late, and the president's staff was anxious to get him to wherever he needed to be next, but President Clinton saw a few National Park Service and concession employees nearby and called them over. He thanked us for the work that we do in managing and protecting Mount Rushmore and our national parks.

Under the twilight blue darkening sky of that balmy evening, he then went on to speak very eloquently about how people of very ordinary means can visit Mount Rushmore and other national park system sites and have the same wonderful experiences that people of great means have. He said that is very democratic and right. I believe that most of us who experienced those few minutes with the president under the lighted sculpture could not help being inspired by his words.

Mike Pflaum
Chief Park Ranger (1989-2008)
Mount Rushmore National Memorial

English Visitors

My wife and I have many memories of having early morning breakfasts at the Memorial before the days of fees, parking garages or modern entrances. We would take our guests, some from foreign countries, up the pristine wandering pathway lined with the state flags to the restaurant. We would try to seek a table nearest the picture window facing the four stone faces.

One couple, Jack and Sheila King, came from Morpeth, England. Of Scottish descent, Jack was in demand as the primary speaker at the annual Robert Burns birthday celebrations. What better way to expose the couple to the American heritage than by taking them to Mount Rushmore!

Reuben and Marloe Bareis
Rapid City, SD

RODGER SLOTT

Sharing "Rount Mushmore"

I was lucky to get to see Mount Rushmore nearly every summer of my childhood because we had a small cabin near Roubaix Lake. My parents would tease me because I always used to ask when we were going to get to see Rount Mushmore! When cousins or friends from out of state would visit us, I was always so proud and excited to show off the monument and to gauge their reactions as they saw it for the first time.

I still enjoy looking for those reactions to this day. It always starts with the anticipation that you see and feel in people who have seen Mount Rushmore in books or advertisements but never before in person. They search for the monument as you drive to it from either direction. Then eyes widen and brighten, mouths open in awe and smiles are quick to fill faces. They get impatient to park the car so they can get out and get closer.

Then come the questions . . . about the history of the place, the sculptor, the carving, the presidents depicted and the park. They've always known it is a place of special meaning for the country, but their own experience in seeing it up close seems to enhance its significance. There always seems to be a certain blend of patriotism and excitement when someone can then say, "I've been to Mount Rushmore!"

Stephanie Herseth Sandlin
U.S. Representative from South Dakota (2004–2010)
Mount Rushmore Society Member
Brookings, SD

Robin Racine poses in front of Mount Rushmore like so many other graduates before and after her.

Local Moments

Stars Shine at Rushmore

My memories of Mount Rushmore go clear back to my growing up years in the little town at the foot of the mountain, Keystone. There I grew up with many of the children whose fathers and sometimes mothers worked at Mount Rushmore. I always loved the summertime when we could walk down to certain places on the highway and look up and see the glow of the faces. Even now, I never get tired of seeing the faces illuminated. It still sends shivers up my spine!

When Cary Grant and the rest of the cast were filming *North by Northwest* in 1959, it was an exciting time in the area. Everyone wanted to see the movie stars! I was waiting tables at the Hi Way Café in Keystone and was lucky enough to be on duty when the crew decided to stop for their coffee break. That made that bright and sunny afternoon just a little brighter!

I spent many Easter services standing outside in the snow, shivering and trying to sing with the Keystone Congregational Church. We would be up by the veranda area or sometimes down in the amphitheater, as it all depended on the amount of snow that covered the ground. Many brave guests and family members stood around to hear the choir sing as they stood under the faces.

We sometimes would travel up to the mountain to hear Allie Hand play the piano and sing in the Buffalo Dining Room. She would play such songs as the "Mount Rushmore Memorial March" and sing such songs as "Take Me Back to the Black Hills," "I Get the Blues for the Black Hills" and our state song, "Hail South Dakota."

Bonita (Mohler Cochran) Ley
Mount Rushmore Society Member
Rapid City, SD

In My Backyard

I moved from Oklahoma to Hill City, South Dakota, when I was 13. My parents built the saw mill there.

As teenagers in high school, we used to go to Mount Rushmore in the summertime just to hang out and people-watch and maybe meet boys. In the wintertime, we would go there and take inner tubes and sled down the old sidewalks. There were never any people around when it was snowing, and it was amazing to have had this experience.

Now I work for the City of Hill City and for Xanterra when they have private parties at Mount Rushmore. It is great fun, and one of the things I like is just being at Mount Rushmore. It is always inspiring to me, no matter how many times I go there.

Brenda J. Shafer
Hill City, SD

Graduation Memories

I graduated from the National Business College in Rapid City in May 1983, and we had our graduation commencement at Mount Rushmore. Little did I know that 21 years later, I would be hired at Mount Rushmore as their budget analyst.

Robin Racine
Prior Budget Analyst
Mount Rushmore National Memorial

Summer Job

I was fortunate enough to land a job with the Youth Conservation Corps (YCC) during the summer between my sophomore and junior years in high school.

My favorite memory from that time was actually going on top of Mount Rushmore and being able to see the Hall of Records, the presidents' faces and the park from a view that very few ever see. I also enjoyed watching one of the maintenance men rappelling down the faces and checking for cracks.

Every month all the employees had a potluck. That was fun. We made homemade ice cream, and the job of turning the ice cream maker by hand fell to us members of the YCC.

It was great to meet people from all over. I feel pride whenever I go back because I know that I helped take care of the monument. It's kind of in my blood.

Larry Maciejewski
Custer, SD

Gutzon Borglum envisioned a grand Hall of Records behind the faces. Although not completed as originally planned, the Hall was finished in 1998 with a vault that contains information on why the mountain was carved, why the presidents were chosen and copies of important American documents. NATIONAL PARK SERVICE

Cabin Fireflies

In 1994, the Goetzinger family purchased a summer cabin in Lafferty Gulch, which lies in the shadow of Mount Rushmore. Since then, we have confirmed that the Goetzinger cabin was built by Mount Rushmore carvers.

While our family's memories are countless, one tradition stands out. We have had a front row seat to the fireworks display every year that it has occurred at the Memorial. Our children have vivid memories of hiking up to the rim to watch and hear the awesome display.

There also must be a connection between fireworks and fireflies. Here is my entry from 1999:

"While the fireworks at the Memorial were spectacular, the fireflies near the Cabin put on an amazing show of Mother Nature's own fireworks. A thousand points of light were dancing in the cool evening air of the open meadow nearest the Cabin. The kids sat on the porch in full giggle watching the 2nd Act of the night."

Another entry revealed my son Nolan's speculation that the glowing beads of light outside the cabin window just had to be the eyes of a mountain lion ready to

pounce. Upon further inspection, we discovered they were just fireflies wanting to entertain us. Much relieved, we settled in to watch their show.

The Goetzinger cabin and Mount Rushmore have been companions to many other memories. They serve as a respite from the challenges of life, a place to reflect and recharge and a place to count our blessings as a family and a nation.

Patrick G. Goetzinger
Mount Rushmore Society Member
Rapid City, SD

AIM at Rushmore

After 43 years at Rushmore, I have so many memories. I started working for Kay Riordan Steuerwald and Jack Riordan, who operated the Mount Rushmore dining room and gift shop, at the age of 18 in 1969. Over the years, I have seen so many changes that it is hard to keep track of them all. My most vivid memory is of the July 4, 1975, march on Rushmore by the American Indian Movement (AIM), and I suppose it is because it is the only July 4th that I have had a day off!

Russ Jobman
General Manager (1993–2014)
Xanterra Parks & Resorts
Mount Rushmore National Memorial

Rain, Rain, Go Away

During my first full summer in Rapid City, a group of close friends visited me from Ohio. Among other things, I took them to the lighting ceremony at Mount Rushmore. This would have been in July of 1976.

That night, the lightning was bouncing around the hills and the thunder was right above our heads. The rain was pouring down in buckets. My friends were determined to stay, and we enjoyed the movie and lighting ceremony all by ourselves. They still comment on how memorable that one special evening was at Mount Rushmore and in the Black Hills.

Patrick H. Wyss
Rapid City, SD

In the Snow

My first visit to the monument was on March 3, 1945, with my parents and brother. It was snowing, a heavy wet March snow. The setting was beautiful.

Ed Hubbeling
Mount Rushmore Society Member
Rapid City, SD

RODGER SLOTT

Mica, Mica

Living here in the Black Hills for 70 years and having the typical influx of visits from family and friends always meant trips to the mountain.

My childhood memories—still vivid—are of climbing around the small hills with my cousins, picking up mica, and bringing it home. We'd split the layers to make all kinds of creations, such as windshields in cars and windows in doll houses. (These were very primitive doll houses!)

Of course, I refer to the original entrance to Mount Rushmore, the public access to all places and the freedom to climb among the rocks and trees

Judy Reedy Olson Duhamel
Mount Rushmore Society Member
Rapid City, SD

Black Hills Gold

World War II had just ended, and my family took a trip to Mount Rushmore. There were gunny sacks of rocks leftover from the faces, so you could bring home a treasure. They even had some bags with shiny flakes. I was sure it was Black Hills gold! Looking at the faces through the binoculars was a thrill.

In the early 1960s, I remember singing "God Bless America" in the dining room during the lighting ceremony, with singing waiters helping us out. We went to Mount Rushmore for dinner every time we had enough money.

Having served as treasurer with the Mount Rushmore Society during the redevelopment of the facilities in the 1990s, I was honored to have my name carved on a granite plaque located on the Grand View Terrace.

Leroy Ketel
Mount Rushmore Society Member
Rapid City, SD

XANTERRA ARCHIVES

Binoculars, once operated by Tower Optical, gave visitors an up-close look at the faces.
XANTERRA ARCHIVES

Laughter

George Clooney

I was asked to read one of our children's books about Mount Rushmore to my niece Brenna's first-grade class. In preparation, the teacher, Mrs. Shloemer, talked to the class about the sculpture and the presidents so it would be a learning experience for all.

As the lively and noisy little class gathered around in preparation for story time, I asked them if they could name the presidents who were featured on Mount Rushmore. I heard, "Abraham Lincoln . . . Thomas Jefferson . . . Roosevelt . . . and George CLOONEY!"

Mrs. Shloemer and I could hardly contain ourselves. "I wish!" she declared.

Diana Nielsen Saathoff, CEO
Mount Rushmore Society
Rapid City, SD

"Mount Mushmore"

My brother's youngest child, Nathan, used to love to go to Mount Rushmore. He would always ask if we all could go. Nathan's father would keep asking, "Where do you want to go?" just to get him to say, "Mount Mushmore."

Judy Cranford
Rapid City, SD

"Polio Girls"

When my sister was a patient at the Hot Springs polio hospital, we drove from Pierre every weekend to visit her. Each trip included a visit to Mount Rushmore for breakfast or lunch. I'm told that as a toddler, I referred to the monument as the "polio girls," a name that persisted in our family for many years. In my defense, Washington and Jefferson did have rather long hair.

Eileen Fleishacker
Mount Rushmore Society Member
Rapid City, SD

Does That Look Right?

If you have visited the Mount Rushmore Bookstores, you have seen "first day" covers on sale. These are sought by collectors who look for the combination of a commemorative postage stamp and an envelope featuring artwork of a celebration or anniversary.

When the Mount Rushmore National Memorial observed its 50th anniversary in 1991, a special "first day" cover went on sale at the mountain. The "first day" covers from this event did not just show up. They were the result of extensive planning by volunteers from the Mount Rushmore Society. With foresight, they realized that someday the covers would be rare and would bring a profit.

The committee secured artwork by Dong Kingman, who was nationally known for his watercolors. A reproduction of his portrayal of Mount Rushmore was printed on thousands of envelopes. Thousands of 29-cent postage stamps were also ordered. Later, the strategically placed postmark would carry the date and these words: "Mount Rushmore, SD, First Day of Issue."

Behind the scenes, approximately 20 Society members volunteered to attach the stamps to the envelopes. Much like a sewing club, the volunteers—all women—gathered in a room provided by the Rapid City Post Office. They developed friendships and became part of an unexpected social group. Fun and banter were part of the process. However, this was a labor-intensive undertaking with strict rules about clean hands and exact placement of each stamp. Always, the focus was on the careful handling of the product.

One day, the usual hum of conversation and assembly work was shattered when one of the ladies excitedly called out, "Oh, I just put two stamps on upside down!" With that announcement, everything came to a noisy halt. Her confession had interrupted hundreds of hours of concentration and accuracy.

That day's session ended in hugs as well as reassurances that she would recover and be welcomed back. However, no one thought to save what might have been a very valuable collector's item today!

Jim Kuehn
Mount Rushmore Society Member
Rapid City, SD

"The Guys"

Several years ago, our family visited Mount Rushmore for the first time. Our daughters, Rachel and Emily, were in awe of the huge monument. We explained to them who each president was and why his head was up on the mountain. Our youngest daughter, Emily, listened carefully to our explanation but then announced that she was just going to call them "the guys."

During our weeklong vacation in the area, Emily wanted to have breakfast every day with "the guys." So we did. As she enjoyed eating her large cinnamon roll, she would look out the window at the monument and announce that she wanted to come back every year to visit "the guys" and eat breakfast with them.

Now Emily has graduated from high school. However, she still refers to our most cherished landmark as "the guys."

Paul and Sandy Compas
Omaha, NE

It's a Small State

One of my first assignments as the education specialist with the National Park Service at Mount Rushmore in 2004 was organizing Read Across America. We were showcased in the national effort as the number one event of 100 events around the country celebrating the birthday of Dr. Seuss and promoting literacy.

Our first attempt to host the event for hundreds of school children was snowed out due to one of South Dakota's notorious spring blizzards. In the face of the growing storm, we scrambled to notify our participants of the cancellation. It occurred to us that we did not have late night contact information for South Dakota First Lady Jean Rounds, who was scheduled to fly out in a state airplane first thing in the morning to participate in the festivities.

On the chance that we might be able to call the governor's mansion directly, Chief of Interpretation Judy Olson called information and asked for the listing for Mr. and Mrs. Rounds of Pierre, South Dakota. A number was quickly provided. When Judy placed the call, the governor answered. Judy asked for Mrs. Rounds, and the governor called out to his wife, "It's for you!"

Now, that's South Dakota!

Rhonda Buell Schier
Education Specialist (2004-2010)
Mount Rushmore National Memorial

The Things People Say

I worked in the log gift shop during the summer of 1956. We were the first summer group to occupy the new dormitory, which was in the area of the current administrative building.

One of my jobs was to sweep the porch in front of the gift shop several times a day while Ben Black Elk stood at one end being photographed by the tourists. While sweeping, I often overheard the tourists telling their kids who was carved on the mountain, and it seemed like they got it wrong as often as right. Franklin Roosevelt was usually up there somewhere!

I especially remember two questions I was asked: "Say, Sonny, what do they do with them in the winter?" And (yes, no kidding), "How far did they have to dig before they found them?"

It was a great summer!

Fred Whiting
Mount Rushmore Society Member
Rapid City, SD

From the Heart

While quizzing a girl for her Junior Ranger badge, I asked her who she should obey when at Mount Rushmore. She immediately answered, "GOD!"

Betty Street
Prior Interpretive Ranger
Mount Rushmore National Memorial

Those Tricky Mountain Goats

Since I oversaw the operations at the Mount Rushmore parking garage, I had to calm down many confused visitors over the years. Two stories stand out.

One visitor, referring to the tracking collars on the wild mountain goats that make the park their home, exclaimed, "It is just awful that you put shock collars on the goats to keep them in the parking lot!"

Concerned about all the mountain goats wandering around, another visitor made sure to alert us that some mountain goats had jumped over the "fences" and needed to be rounded up again.

Bob Mudlin
President (1998–2016)
Presidential Parking, Inc.
Mount Rushmore National Memorial

Overheard at Mount Rushmore

"DAD, COME OUT HERE! COME SEE THIS YAK!"

"DO YOU HAVE POLAR BEARS HERE?"

"WHAT DID YOU DO WITH THE LAURA INGALLS WILDER HOUSE THAT USED TO BE HERE?"

"WHERE DO YOU GO TO TAKE PICTURES OUT OF THE EYES?"

"WHEN DID YOU GUYS ADD THE FOURTH FACE? I WAS HERE AWHILE AGO AND THERE WERE ONLY THREE!"

"WHERE'S OLD FAITHFUL?"

"THE PARKING GARAGE IS BECAUSE OF THE WATERGATE SCANDAL."

In case you're wondering …

Mount Rushmore National Memorial does not have yaks or polar bears. However, it is home to several shaggy, white mountain goats.

There was never a Laura Ingalls Wilder house at Mount Rushmore. However, her sister Carrie lived in Keystone.

You cannot take pictures out of the eyes because the faces are not hollow. They are made of solid granite.

All four faces (including Roosevelt's) were carved between 1927 and 1941.

Old Faithful is located at Yellowstone National Park in Wyoming. However, you can find natural hot water in Hot Springs, South Dakota, just 50 miles south of Mount Rushmore.

The parking garage is not the result of Richard Nixon or the Watergate Scandal. In the 1990s, private citizens raised $57 million to renovate the visitor and parking facilities.

Photos taken by photographer Roland Nohlgren when he worked for The Journal, *now called the* Rapid City Journal.

Rare Views

Rushmore in Pictures

My father, Roland F. Nohlgren, worked as an engraver and photographer for *The Journal* from 1937 to 1943.

His passion was photography. He almost always developed the film himself. I think that was part of the fun for my dad. He thoroughly enjoyed going to Mount Rushmore to take pictures of progress on the monument. He wasn't afraid to climb around on the "faces" with the workmen. Indeed, he was a great admirer of Borglum and invited him to our home for dinner at least once that I can remember.

My parents loved the Black Hills. They had such fond memories of the camera club get-togethers, horseback trips to Harney Peak, picnics in the pines and road trips through the Needles. I remember that period as being a very happy time for my parents.

Sonia Hunter
Mount Rushmore Archives

Flying Whirlybirds

My love affair with Mount Rushmore began in 1961 when I was one of the three owners of Whirlybirds over Mount Rushmore. I was chosen to be in charge for the next four years. I carried thousands of people, accident-free, over Mount Rushmore, giving them "A Sight and Experience You Will Never Forget." The ride went just a few feet over Washington's head, which was quite a thrill. We waved to the crowds on the patio below from the open door of my helicopter. The people would wave back while Allie Hand played on the organ "Cruising Over Rushmore in My Little Helicopter."

As time went on, I flew farther away from the monument, which wasn't as much fun for the passengers, but I was happy to accommodate the wishes of the Mount Rushmore staff.

John Sundby
Mount Rushmore Society Member
Rapid City, SD

Whirlybirds over Mount Rushmore in 1961. STAR TRIBUNE

Tail No. 637, Pix @ Rushmore

During my second tour in the Air Force, I was assigned to Ellsworth Air Force Base as a T-38 instructor pilot. Almost every day we would fly by Mount Rushmore on our way home from our training area near Edgemont to "show the flag," make a little jet noise (the Sound of Freedom), and rock the wings to wave hi to the visitors.

In the summer of 1990, we were granted permission for a four-ship flyby of the monument for a photo opportunity.

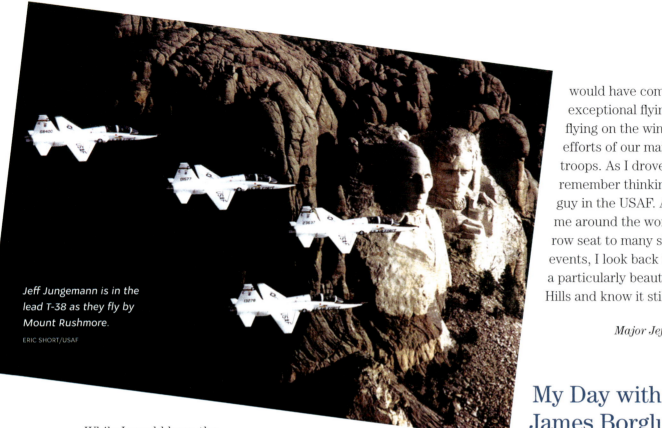

Jeff Jungemann is in the lead T-38 as they fly by Mount Rushmore.
ERIC SHORT/USAF

would have come to pass without the exceptional flying skill of the other pilots flying on the wing and the tremendous efforts of our maintenance and support troops. As I drove home that night, I can remember thinking I had to be the luckiest guy in the USAF. After a career that took me around the world and gave me a front row seat to many significant places and events, I look back to a very special flight on a particularly beautiful morning in the Black Hills and know it still to be true.

Major Jeff Jungemann, USAF, Retired
Cordova, MD

My Day with James Borglum

While I would have the privilege of leading the formation, the challenging task of flying #4 at the "end of the whip" was given to one of our best instructor pilots, Ted Davis. Eric Short, a fellow instructor pilot, would snap the pictures from the rear cockpit of the chase ship.

As we climbed out from Ellsworth just before sunrise, I looked back at the other jets lifting off in succession and could see the blue flames from their afterburners marking their haste to rejoin and form up. We made several passes that morning, and I can remember seeing the parking area flash by below us. I suspect that our sudden arrival on the scene at 350 mph probably caused a coffee cup or two to be spilled. And although I probably had one of the best views of the presidents since Mr. Borglum, I don't remember seeing any of the faces as we went by, so concentrated was I on hitting my marks and keeping us out of the trees and rocks. I do remember thinking that I did not want to be remembered as the guy who put a dent in Mount Rushmore.

My logbook for that day only notes "Tail No. 637, Pix @ Rushmore"—apparently just another routine day. But it truly was a once in a lifetime opportunity that never

One of my closest friends and longtime business partners is James "Jim" G. Borglum, the grandson of Gutzon Borglum and son of Lincoln Borglum. Back in the days when security wasn't quite the issue that it is now, the Borglum family was allowed access to venture to the top of the Memorial regularly. On one occasion, Jim asked if I would like to go with him. Since I had never had the opportunity to go on top of the faces, I jumped at the chance.

When the day arrived, Jim brought along his father's old Kodak camera that still had a partially used roll of film in it from before his father had passed away, many years prior. Jim wanted to check and see if the film was still any good. Because it still had a few shots left, he took the remaining shots of me on top of the presidents' heads.

Later that night, I was overwhelmed. Just having had the opportunity to go on top of Mount Rushmore was in itself an amazing experience. But it was so much more. I had the grandson of the creator of Mount Rushmore as my tour guide. I had my picture taken by an old camera owned by Lincoln Borglum which still had film in it (with other undeveloped pictures taken by Lincoln himself), and I listened to Jim's stories of the many trips up the mountain with his father. It was truly an unbelievable, surreal experience.

The film was still good, and when Jim had it developed, he gave me the black-and-white photos snapped that day on top of the faces. One photo, which shows me standing on top of George's head looking off into never-never land, is a family favorite.

Phil Lampert
Mount Rushmore Society Member
Custer, SD

Get That Goat!

As the senior photographer for the South Dakota Office of Tourism, I have visited and photographed Mount Rushmore thousands of times. This picture of a mountain goat at Mount Rushmore is one of my favorites of all time and has appeared in many publications and websites.

People often want to know exactly where the picture was taken, so here's the story. It may not appear so, but the photo was taken in the parking garage area of Mount Rushmore.

As a matter of fact, it took quite a while to get things lined up. I wanted the sculptured faces behind the goat, but I didn't want to have cars driving through the image as they made their way between the two parking garages.

A telephoto lens made the goat and the Rushmore faces appear as if they were closer together than they really were. Here's an illustration (to the right) of where I was and where the goat was standing.

Chad Coppess
Pierre, SD

The 1991 Golden Anniversary Dedication of Mount Rushmore National Memorial.
NATIONAL PARK SERVICE

Ceremonies and Celebrations

Honored to Serve

My father, Lyle Edwards, was born in 1929, the year which began the Great Depression. As a young child attending a one-room schoolhouse in the Genesee River Valley of northwestern Pennsylvania, he recalls collecting precious pennies to contribute toward the sculpting of Mount Rushmore. He often dreamed of traveling to South Dakota to see this magnificent tribute to four of America's most revered presidents, but as a poor country boy, he never thought he would.

At the age of 17, Lyle determined that his best opportunity to leave the farm and see the world was to join the U.S. Army. His assignment took him to Japan and later to Korea. Soon after his return to the States, he married his high school sweetheart, and they began to raise their family of three children. I was one of them.

In 1977, I traveled to the Black Hills to spend the summer with friends and fell in love with a man from Rapid City. We were engaged within a week. Surprisingly, my parents had no reservations about our engagement. Instead, my father said, "I have ALWAYS wanted to see Mount Rushmore. You two make arrangements for a South Dakota wedding, and we will be there."

Six weeks later, they arrived at the airport. Of course, our first stop was Mount Rushmore. My father was awed by its magnificence. He was more tearful on the mountain than he was at our wedding!

Over the years, my parents have made more visits to Mount Rushmore. My most poignant memory was in the summer of 2006 when we were able to spend Independence Day together at the mountain. The director of the Air Force Band invited retired military personnel to stand as the band played their particular theme song.

As my father stood for the Army song, I told him how proud and grateful I was for his service. Once again, his tears of patriotism flowed freely in front of Mount Rushmore.

Kathy Simpson
Rapid City, SD

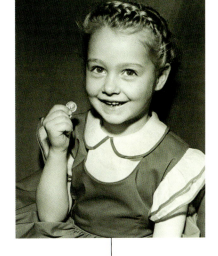

In the 1930s, the Mount Rushmore Society organized a fundraiser in which school children were encouraged to donate change for the Mount Rushmore carving. In all, $1,707.80 was collected.

Golden Anniversary

The final dedication came on July 3, 1991, with a program to celebrate the completion of Mount Rushmore fifty years ago.

There were many dignitaries present for the celebration. Both of the U.S. senators were in attendance, Tom Daschle and Larry Pressler. Those participating in the show from Hollywood and television were Jimmy Stewart, Rosemary Clooney and Barbara Eden. I had the pleasure and privilege of shaking hands with Jimmy Stewart. President George H.W. Bush gave the principal

Flag-folding ceremonies are performed nightly during the Evening Lighting Ceremony. This one honored three WWII Lakota Code Talkers on July 3, 2009. RODGER SLOTT

address at the dedication ceremony. The co-emcees were Tom Brokaw and Mary Hart, both born and raised in South Dakota.

I have been fortunate and privileged to have had the opportunity to gather so many memories of Mount Rushmore that will never be equaled or surpassed.

Bob Hayes
Keystone, SD

Reunions

Independence Day 2008 was a long-awaited vacation and reunion of Vietnam Army vets who hadn't seen each other for 40 years. We met with our wives at a hotel near Mount Rushmore for a reunion time before attending the traditional Independence Day ceremonies held at "the faces" on July 3rd.

Imagine our emotions while the emcee described how we—veterans from South Dakota, Iowa, Texas, Pennsylvania, Ohio and New York—hadn't had contact with each other for 40 years except through Christmas cards and emails, and that we had decided to reunite during this most appropriate holiday at this site that emanated patriotism.

The welcome from the crowd, the patriotic fervor and the flyover by the big bombers had our hearts in our throats and tears in our eyes as we looked upon the stone faces of the men who made this country great. This is a Mount Rushmore memory that we will never forget.

Howard Rupp
Cleghorn, IA

Veterans

During the July 4th week of 2008, I coordinated a reunion of six fellow Army buddies from my time spent in Vietnam. The majority of our group maintained contact with each other through the years with Christmas cards, but many of us had not seen each other since our tour of duty ended in 1968.

I was very fortunate to have excellent cooperation from various individuals to have passes for an early entry to the Amphitheater for the fireworks event. Without my six buddies knowing, I had arranged with Dr. Sid Goss, emcee for the event, to recognize us during the evening.

My friend, Sid, positively honored my request. The pride in each of us when asked to stand to be recognized was overwhelming. The pride of serving our country was made much greater by celebrating our 40th reunion at Mount Rushmore.

Lloyd W. Sohl
Mount Rushmore Society Member
Rapid City, SD

Foggy Fireworks

The first Independence Day Celebration & Fireworks event was held in 1999. The fireworks had been scheduled for midnight of July 3, so that the second it became July 4, they would go off. Dense fog moved in, and one fireworks' shell was fired. It made a red glow in the cloud, but that was it. The show was postponed until the evening of July 5 when it went off without a hitch and was beautiful.

Chad Coppess
Pierre, SD

Emcee Memories

I have many memories from my years as emcee of the Mount Rushmore fireworks celebration.

Robert Moore was the Native American opera singer who sang the "Battle Hymn of the Republic" and "God Bless America" as part of the event. We coordinated his singing so that he would hit and hold his last note at exactly the same time that a B-52 flew over Mount Rushmore.

I recall one time when the plane was going too slowly. I remember hearing the Air Force officer (who sat off stage) shouting into his radio, "Hit it! Hit it!" In the distance, I could see the exhaust as the pilot "put the hammer down" in order to come in on top of Robert's final note. Of course, there was a greater noise from the plane than usual . . . as well as a greater amount of excitement from the crowd.

Robert Moore was always delighted when we could coordinate everything. If a jet drowned out his last note, it was perfect.

Other memories were more solemn.

Before the fireworks display, an Air Force flag-folding team would conduct a flag-folding ceremony. As emcee, I would read a description of the ceremony and its meaning, and the flag would be given to a member of the United States military. I also had the honor of reading aloud the biography of the recipient. Often, there was not a dry eye in the audience.

I remember three of these recipients quite well: Clarence Wolf Guts, the last living Lakota code talker; Jack van der Geest, one of only eight to have ever escaped from the Buchenwald concentration camp; and Frank Buckles, the last living survivor from World War I. He was 107 years old.

Sid Goss
Mount Rushmore Society Member
Emcee of the Independence Day
Celebration & Fireworks event (1999-2009)
Deadwood, SD

People in the Amphitheater await the Independence Day Celebration on July 3 circa 2005. SOUTH DAKOTA TOURISM

Booms

I have many wonderful memories at Mount Rushmore. My husband and I convinced his family to brave the crowds and attend the fireworks on July 3rd. The day was filled with terrific entertainment in the Amphitheater with acts that were fun for the kids (and the kids at heart), as well as with military bands and their amazing patriotic music.

Just before the fireworks, "God Bless America" was sung by a gentleman with the most beautiful voice. I looked at my mother-in-law, and she had tears rolling down her cheeks.

Then the B-1 flew over and the fireworks began. Our nephew and niece, who were five and three at the time, were looking up with the biggest saucer eyes ever. You could have put a baseball in their open mouths! Afterward, as we were driving home, they were almost shouting over each other to say how awesome it was and how their pants were still shaking from the "booms."

My favorite part of the fireworks show was the silence that followed the grand finale. It was a "did we just see, hear and feel what we think we did??" moment.

Dawn Miller
Summerset, SD

SALLIE TAYLOR ZAMBELLI

Happy Birthday, Mr. President

My first Independence Day Celebration & Fireworks as president of the Mount Rushmore Society was a memorable experience. On the evening of July 3, 2009, the Memorial was full of people for the annual fireworks show. It was very foggy, and fireworks were delayed. Everyone hoped for the skies to clear.

Superintendent Gerard Baker, along with several leaders and myself, were down at the Amphitheater stalling for time. Knowing that my birthday was on July 4, Superintendent Baker asked me to join him on the stage. Next, he led the entire crowd in singing "Happy Birthday" to me. That was a wonderful 70th birthday gift and one I will never forget.

The fireworks went off. However, due to the fog, it was probably the world's largest man-made Northern Lights show in history!

Gene Lebrun
Mount Rushmore Society Member
Rapid City, SD

Meeting a WWI Veteran

When I was a kid growing up in Murdo, South Dakota, going on vacation meant getting in the car and heading west to the Black Hills for Labor Day weekend. Like most families, we didn't go every year, but I remember going to see the faces with my parents and sometimes staying for the awe-inspiring lighting ceremony at night.

As a father, I remember taking my own daughters to Mount Rushmore on many occasions, but the celebrations surrounding Independence Day were a family favorite. Watching our daughters' faces as they looked up at the former presidents they had read about in their history

WWI veteran Frank Buckles recognized for military service during a flag-folding ceremony on July 3, 2008. DEBBIE SPEAS

books was always a moment of great joy for my wife, Kimberley, and me.

As a U.S. senator in 2008, I was honored to spend a day at Mount Rushmore with Frank Buckles, who at the time was 107 and the last remaining World War I veteran. It doesn't get much better than celebrating Independence Day at the Shrine of Democracy with an American hero.

John Thune
U.S. Senator from South Dakota
Sioux Falls, SD

Naturalization Ceremony

On the morning of June 14, 1991 (Flag Day), I took the oath as a new citizen of the United States of America at Mount Rushmore.

It was a perfect Black Hills summer day with bright blue skies and a gentle breeze. The thrill and sense of excitement of realizing that life, liberty and the pursuit of happiness were my rights was amplified by the presence of Presidents George Washington, Thomas Jefferson, Abraham Lincoln and Teddy Roosevelt.

Reflecting back 20 years, I believe becoming a U.S. citizen at Mount Rushmore made me a better American; it was a glaring reminder that the greatness of our nation is the result of ordinary people who take on monumental challenges, often against all odds.

Since then, I have made the trip to Mount Rushmore countless times. While so much in our country and the world has changed, one thing that doesn't change with each visit is my sense of pride of being a citizen of this great nation and my pledge to never take America for granted as long as I live.

Qusi Al-Haj
Rapid City, SD

More than 100 people from 36 countries became citizens of the United States during this 2011 Naturalization Ceremony held at Mount Rushmore National Memorial. DEBBIE SPEAS

Mary, Mary Ellis, Gutzon and Lincoln Borglum. Lincoln's daughter, Robin Borglum Carter, is pictured in the inset photo, enjoying a day at the mountain.

NATIONAL PARK SERVICE

Reflections

Borglum Family Memories

My earliest experiences at Mount Rushmore were not really memories but family lore. My parents, Louella and Lincoln Borglum, took me—their six-month-old baby—on one of the last cable car trips up the mountain, just before everything was dismantled. Then there were stories of park rangers assigned to watch over me as I clamored around the rocks near the trails when dad was working as superintendent. A not-so-flattering story was told about me being stopped by my irate father from trying to sell autographs to tourists!

The mountain was always in the background of our life no matter where we lived. Dad wrote books about his own and his father, Gutzon Borglum's, experiences at the mountain; he gave interviews and speeches while pursuing his own sculpting, ranching and other interests; and he delighted in telling stories about the early years of carving a mountain in South Dakota.

It wasn't until many years later, after Dad died in 1986, that I had more direct contact with the mountain itself, the people who worked there and the Mount Rushmore Society.

Gradually, the building improvements at the mountain during the 1990s took priority in my life, as my brother Jim and Aunt Mary Ellis Borglum Vhay became involved in promoting the Hall of Records. We took on the task of making it a part of Mount Rushmore's interpretive plan over the next decade, following through on the dream that Gutzon Borglum, Mary Borglum and my dad had cherished long ago.

That involvement led to understanding the commitment and dreams represented by those carved heads and encouraged me to give speeches and write a book about Gutzon's other artworks entitled, *Gutzon Borglum: His Life and Works*.

Some other poignant memories are:

… a bugle playing Taps from the darkness of the mountain at Dad's memorial service.

… the incredible trip to the top for the dedication of the Hall of Records and my privilege of inviting individuals to come forward to place a panel in the time capsule.

… speaking about Dad at the dedication of the new Lincoln Borglum Museum & Visitor Center with all my family present.

… developing friendships with National Park Service personnel and the families of some of the original workers.

… listening to visitors tell inspiring stories of why they visited the mountain, such as the Make-A-Wish child who wanted to see Mount Rushmore more than anything, an elderly military man making his last trip across America and the many foreign visitors who equate those carved heads with the United States of America and democracy.

Mary Ellis Borglum Vhay with members of the National Park Service at the Hall of Records Dedication.
NATIONAL PARK SERVICE

At first, Mount Rushmore was just where my dad worked. Much later, it became who I was, too. Only later, when I was inadvertently there a few days after 9/11 and saw the spontaneous tributes of flowers and notes at the base of the state flag poles, did I begin to truly sense that these four presidents had seen things in our country as evil as the Twin Tower devastation. They had persevered, and we would, too.

I was in the audience during the Evening Lighting Ceremony. Tears streamed down our faces as we all sought solace and answers from this powerful symbol of our country. I was touched by the capacity of the Memorial to reflect both stability and hope for our future.

We have faced significant challenges in the past, and there will always be future ones, but Mount Rushmore is a reminder of what America can accomplish. Our history speaks to our future.

Robin Borglum Kennedy
Mount Rushmore Society Member
Galveston, TX

The Last Christmas

Borglum always called his employees by their last name, and he treated the families very graciously, including the children. I recall attending banquets at the boarding house at the mountain and the Alex Johnson Hotel, and picnics at the Borglum ranch near Hermosa.

Borglum hosted a Christmas party for families and children in the old studio at Mount Rushmore in 1940. My mother, four-year-old sister and I attended. Dad was not there, but I later learned he was hidden behind a white beard and red suit. This was Borglum's last Christmas on earth. Borglum passed away in a Chicago hospital from an embolism on March 6, 1941.

Shortly after his death, there was a memorial service for Borglum at the Keystone Congregational Church. The Rushmore workers entered the church in a group. Alton "Hoot" Leach called off each worker's name as they entered, which was very impressive. Keystone Boy Scout Troop #50 acted as an honor guard. I was finally a Boy Scout, and I was in uniform.

Bob Hayes
Keystone, SD

Morning Awe

We are early risers and could hardly wait to start our first day of vacation in the Black Hills. Number one on our list: watching the sun rise over Mount Rushmore.

We drove up Highway 244 in the dark, parked our car and walked up to the main promenade. Standing less than 10 feet from us, just off the sidewalk, were three mountain goats, peacefully grazing. We stood all alone in the center of the viewing terrace, sipping our coffee in the morning silence as the sun slowly began its ascent. For us, there was a magic in the solitude.

Growing up in the Midwest, we'd taken our freedoms for granted, but seeing the monument for the first time was a humbling and inspiring moment. In that quiet, crisp morning in May, we stood next to one another, allowing the power and majesty of the monument and the freedom it represents to wash over us.

Little did we know that Mount Rushmore would become an integral part of our lives. Within one year, we moved from southern Minnesota to make Hill City our new home. Within one more year, my husband accepted a position at Mount Rushmore. Now in our tenth year in the Black Hills, we have been honored to have some of our artwork on permanent display in the Mount Rushmore dining room and to have hosted our daughter's wedding at the base of our beloved monument.

Still, we occasionally take pause in our busy lives to stand at the base of the carving. We remember that special first morning when we stood on the terrace in silent awe, each time feeling that powerful emotion of gratitude wash over us.

Jennifer and Dean Karschnik
Hill City, SD

Four Days of Reflection

My husband, who does not like to fly, wanted to take me to see Mount Rushmore. I asked him why since I knew his fear. He said, "Because you always wanted to see it." So we took the trip during the summer of 2006.

When we were driving into the parking lot, I kept my eyes closed as I wanted my first impression to be truly grand. When I walked up the pathway, seeing all the flags and finally seeing the magnificent monument, I cried. It was the one place in the world that I had always wanted to visit.

During our visit, we experienced the evening light show. It was truly moving and patriotic. I was proud to be an American. We spent four days at Mount Rushmore. People asked us, "Why so many days?" Much of the time my husband and I would sit in the Amphitheater and just look at the presidents and reflect. It was an amazing sight.

Constance Grando
Baldwin, NY

A Public Servant's Memories

During my years of public service, I have had numerous opportunities to attend special events at the Shrine of Democracy. I especially remember the 50th anniversary observance, which included President George H.W. Bush, actor Jimmy Stewart, singer Rosemary Clooney and many of the favorite sons and daughters of South Dakota.

I've also attended the Independence Day fireworks, hosted cabinet-level secretaries on their visits to the beautiful Black Hills and had the pleasure of attending the special functions of the Mount Rushmore Society. I was also pleased to work with delegation members, the Mount Rushmore Society and National Park Service officials years ago to raise funds through commemorative coin legislation for the renovation of the Shrine's facilities.

But one of my most cherished memories at Mount Rushmore was attending a naturalization ceremony to swear in America's newest citizens. I also had the opportunity to greet Scouts in the Amphitheater and to present a Purple Heart, Bronze Star and Silver Star to a Vietnam veteran.

With each visit, I have been greatly motivated by the enormity of the work and challenges faced by sculptor Gutzon Borglum and the hundreds of local workers who built the Shrine.

Mount Rushmore stands as a fitting tribute to the greatness of our American democracy as well as to our veterans and soldiers and to the generations of hardworking Americans whose ideals, values and traditions are collectively preserved and immortalized in the Shrine's presentation of Washington, Roosevelt, Jefferson and Lincoln.

Tim Johnson
U.S. Senator from
South Dakota
(1997–2014)
Vermillion, SD

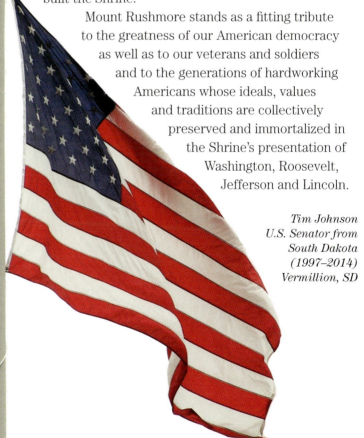

Reflections on Perseverance

An idea is a funny thing. It comes out of nowhere and takes a life of its own. Much like Mount Rushmore. The initial idea for Mount Rushmore did not center around creating a "Shrine of Democracy," but rather creating a tourism attraction. In the same way, the initial idea for creating a public/private partnership for Mount Rushmore improvements over 25 years ago was not spurred by public concern, but rather a call from Charlton Heston. Well, kind of.

In the mid-1980s, the National Park Service had identified the need for $16 to $20 million dollars in improvements to make the facilities more accessible and to accommodate growing visitation. One day, I received a call from a representative for Charlton Heston, who was looking for a project that Heston could put his name behind as a "celebrity chair." I began discussions with the Mount Rushmore Society to see if they would be interested in partnering to raise money for this project. At that time, the Society was a small organization, providing support to Mount Rushmore on a variety of small projects. It was without an executive director and had $100,000 in the bank.

Within six months, Heston decided not to participate, but by this time a fire had been ignited within this group of concerned citizens, headed by Society President Carolyn Mollers. The Society's board of directors had already been talking to South Dakota's governor and congressional leaders and had garnered support.

So they found another well-known campaign chairman in Al Neuharth of *USA Today*, hired an executive director and a development director, and embarked on a multimillion-dollar fundraising campaign. The campaign included selling commemorative stamps, coins and other products, as well as implementing a huge Golden Anniversary Dedication Ceremony in 1991 with President George H. W. Bush and other celebrities in attendance.

A view of the redevelopment accomplished by the fortitude of local citizens in the 1990s to update facilities and increase accessibility to Mount Rushmore National Memorial. JOHNNY SUNDBY

REPRINTED WITH PERMISSION FROM THE ARGUS LEADER.

By 1994 or so, the Mount Rushmore Society had raised about 30 million dollars. However, the redevelopment project had grown to just under 60 million dollars. I remember one pivotal meeting of this fundraising committee. They were trying to determine how they could raise more money and were looking at the many options before them. None were easy or offered a guarantee of success.

In the middle of the discussions, I asked to speak and told them that they already had accomplished what no one thought they could. They had raised 30 million dollars, had brought national attention to Mount Rushmore and had even gotten the president of the United States involved. I gave them a way out by saying, "If you stop now, you have already succeeded."

There was a moment of silence, and then Clifford Grace, the national campaign treasurer, looked at me and said, "The men and women in this room are not used to failing at anything. We will raise the money." And they did.

To see that kind of commitment and passion to complete a vision was extraordinary! It was the kind of commitment and passion that carved Mount Rushmore, and it is the kind of commitment and passion that many Americans have as they make their portion of the world the best it can be.

Dan Wenk
Superintendent (1985-2001)
Mount Rushmore National Memorial
Mount Rushmore Society Member

Evening Lighting Ceremony on September 12, 2001.
NATIONAL PARK SERVICE

9/11

On 9/11, I was in the South Dakota governor's office, watching the events of the day unfold. We were receiving calls from the Pentagon, updating us on the steps the national government was taking to make sure that national landmarks were secure. Mount Rushmore was near the top of the list. If attacked, it would be a very symbolic hit at the core of America.

When things settled down a few weeks later, the governor and I took a trip to Mount Rushmore. I think it was the first time that I really realized what the Memorial meant to our country.

I remember walking up the steps and looking up at the Memorial, realizing that their faces and their history represent an enduring symbol of freedom, not just for our own country, but for the rest of the world.

James D. Hagen
Secretary of Tourism
South Dakota Department of Tourism
Pierre, SD

Day of Renewal

We all remember where we were on 9/11. I happened to be at home, getting ready for my day at work at Mount Rushmore. I heard the reports of the attacks on the World Trade towers, later to find out that the Pentagon had been hit and that Flight 93 had been bound for the White House.

Mount Rushmore shut down for the day. Not knowing how widespread the attack would be, we brought in law enforcement rangers to provide security. I was teamed up with someone from Wind Cave National Park through the night of September 11 and through the morning of September 12.

On my first shift, I wandered the property as the sun went down. We looked in every nook and cranny of every building and in the parking lot, searching for things that were out of place or could be considered threats. At the same time, a shift was on duty on top of the mountain, looking for air threats to the sculpture.

My shift on top of the sculpture was from midnight to 4:00 a.m. on the morning of September 12. For four hours, I sat on top of George Washington's head, looking out across the landscape and across the physical skyline. For four hours, I thought about what had gone on the day before. I had lots of time to contemplate and to think about how our country would change.

Mount Rushmore was open the next day to visitors. At the lighting ceremony that evening, I invited all 800 of the folks who were there to move to the front of the Amphitheater to bond together. Then I delivered the program. It was a powerful night.

I focused on the setbacks in the lives of the four presidents and how they turned these setbacks into opportunities. Our country also had been hit by a setback, a setback of the gravest nature. But even though the setback had rocked the foundations of our cities, it had not rocked the foundations of our people. Our unity and strength were secure.

I suggested that we not look at the tragedy as a setback, but as an opportunity to renew our commitment to the ideals of freedom and liberty, and as an opportunity to make our country stronger.

Afterwards, people lingered at the sculpture for about two or three hours. It gave all of us a time to reflect and to think about how we had changed and how the nation had changed. September 11 had been the watershed, but September 12 was the first day of renewal.

Blaine Kortemeyer
Deputy Director of Interpretation and Education
Mount Rushmore National Memorial

In the Crowd

We were at Mount Rushmore the first day it reopened after 9/11, and the park person who did the ceremony that night was incredible. His invitation to have people move down, be closer together in light of the previous day's activities, and then his moving story of overcoming challenges in his life and the smooth transition into the need for the United States to overcome challenges was excellent.

I have told the story of that night so many times, and I still can't tell it without tears in my eyes. The night was cool and clear, the Big Dipper was sitting right on top of the four faces, the speaker was outstanding and my precious daughter was curled upon my lap, with my husband and dad on either side of me. It was the perfect place to be and an outstanding service to the events of 9/11.

I know that everyone says they will remember where they were during that time, but the experience we had at Mount Rushmore that evening goes way beyond remembering where we were. It was a life-altering experience.

Ann Lechelt
Waunakee, WI

RODGER SLOTT (BACKGROUND)

Looking Ahead

Past, Present and Future

My wife, Terry, and I saved and prepared for nearly eight years before setting off with our boys—Luke, 13 and Jake, eight—on an RV trip across our great country in 2008. Hailing from Boston, historical sites are part of our everyday landscape. Yet arriving at Mount Rushmore on Independence Day was one of the most patriotic experiences of my life.

My family entered the park on the most glorious day of the year. The blue from the sky reflected the clear midday light and washed everything clean. We'd never seen a sky so big before. The festive atmosphere engulfed us. Separated from my family to purchase some sugary treats, I paused to listen to the beautifully haunting rhythms of an indigenous group. The drums bellowed softly, supporting the high melody of a pitch-whistle, both drawn together by the chanting of a striking Native American man.

This became the soundtrack of one of the most profound moments of my life. I spotted my family laughing and jostling each other, communing with their fellow citizens at this sacred American shrine. Then I looked up and caught my first real glimpse of the magnificent structure dwarfing them, watching over us all. I could see the past, present and future of our country and of my own family in a single, joy-filled, sacred moment.

Ted Witherell
Walpole, MA

Our Continuing Story

I grew up in the shadows of Mount Rushmore and have been around it all my life. I have vague memories of being in the old, old concession building, which was where the Borglum View Terrace now sits. I have attended presidential visits at Mount Rushmore, various dedications, awe-inspiring fireworks and incredible flybys. I have known superintendents and staff and met one of the last-living WWI veterans and one of the few female pilots from WWII. I have hiked and jeeped places where you can no longer hike or jeep.

Of the rich tapestry of amazing memories I have of Mount Rushmore, the one that stands out occurred just a couple of years ago when I had the opportunity to speak to a group of people who had chosen to renounce the countries of their birth and become citizens of the United States during a naturalization ceremony. These people valued their naturalized citizenship more than many of us natives even take the time to consider. There were young and old, singles and couples. There were several wearing the uniform of our armed services. Imagine that! The terrace was full of families and friends, all bursting with joy and pride in support of those being naturalized.

To me, the most heart-wrenching moment was when I saw an old friend of my mother's. She was from Thailand and had worked as an aide at a nursing home my mother supervised 40 years ago. Finally, she was becoming a citizen. Her whole family was there, and she was elated, full of the joy of having at last what most of us take for granted: citizenship of the greatest nation on earth.

The new citizens stood under the steadfast gaze of four of our most beloved presidents. What an appropriate place to welcome those who will be part of the continuing story of our greatness!

J. Allan Johnson
Mount Rushmore Society Member
Hill City, SD

Records for the Future

The Borglum family sponsored the placement of historical documents in the Hall of Records on top of the monument. At a dedication ceremony in 1998, I was honored to be asked to lower one of the metal cylinders containing such documents into a hole in the floor of the Hall of Records, which was then sealed. These records will last thousands of years. I often wonder what some scientist or historian a thousand years from now will think of those documents and the period of time that my generation lived on our planet.

James S. Nelson
Mount Rushmore Society Member
Rapid City, SD

The Quiet Landscape

The trees, the wildlife and the landscape are integral to the memory of Mount Rushmore. The preservation of Mount Rushmore is not just about protecting the sculpture but also the setting in which it sits.

Bruce Weisman
Prior Curator
Mount Rushmore National Memorial

Just Keep Going

I remember the day a group of rangers explored some of the upper ranges near Mount Rushmore with Chief Ranger Don Hart. We climbed granite outcroppings, we shimmied through narrow passageways, we pulled ourselves up on ropes and we jumped over crevices.

When we returned to lower ground at the end of our tour, I looked up at some of the areas where we faced those challenges, and I asked Don, "How did you know we could do those things we didn't know we could do?"

"Because you didn't say you couldn't," Don said. "When I showed you where we were headed and what we were going to do next, if you had said, 'I can't do that,' we

RODGER SLOTT

would have turned around and come back. As long as you didn't say, 'I can't do that' we kept going."

Just keep going. That's what George Washington did creating a government. That's what Thomas Jefferson did expanding a nation. That's what Abraham Lincoln did preserving the union. That's what Theodore Roosevelt did building a modern country. That's what Gutzon Borglum did carving a mountain, and that's what everyday citizens do as they follow their dreams.

Rhonda Buell Schier
Education Specialist (2004-2010)
Mount Rushmore National Memorial

Mount Rushmore Speaks

Carved deep on Rushmore's lofty, rugged peak
Are more than silent visages of stone.
In eloquence their chiseled lips bespeak
The noblest creeds mankind has ever known:
A faith in God, at Valley Forge expressed;
Fierce claim of independence for man's soul;
Respect for nature's gifts, her rich bequest;
Man's worth and dignity, his rightful role.

And as our eyes are upward drawn to view
That matchless work of art, we taller stand
And pray, "Oh God, within our hearts renew
Those creeds that once preserved and shaped our land.
And may our Nation in those virtues trust
Till Rushmore's granite might returns to dust."

Miss Nicy Murphy
Amarillo, TX

Miss Nicy Murphy served the great state of South Dakota as its Women's Missionary Union pioneer missionary/director from 1955 to 1976. She celebrated her 100th birthday on May 16, 2011.

RODGER SLOTT

Postcard:
"It's Not 'The End'! My husband and I are retired and travel with our grandchildren. This was a 'west' trip. I must say we are going to come back..."
Laura Osterland
Edinburg, OH.

Mt. Rushmore Society
P.O. Box 1524
Rapid City, SD 57

Coolidge hands over a tool for drilling to sculptor Gutzon Borglum during a Mount Rushmore Dedication Ceremony on August 10, 1927.
LINCOLN BORGLUM COLLECTION

More to Remember

Since *Mount Rushmore Memories* was first published in 2010, more people have submitted memories. They speak to how Mount Rushmore brings individuals together, and they remind us of details that could easily be forgotten over time. In honor of keeping the memories alive, the following voices add to the Mount Rushmore story.

Memories of the Sons

I was only a toddler when my dad, Orville Worman, was working on the mountain. My memories are a bit fuzzy, but my dad and mom shared stories of his time working on the mountain and playing shortstop for the Rushmore Memorial Baseball Team. I still have the flannel ball boy uniform that I wore to games. It hangs on my wall.

As a young boy, I was unaware of the significance of his work. As the project progressed and the mountain was transformed into a monument, it became increasingly apparent that he was a part of something important. I see it as Borglum intended. A homage to great leadership. A lasting reminder of our country's greatness. A bold, giant awe-inspiring artistic achievement.

For me, Rushmore has provided a source of immense pride throughout my entire life.

Richard Worman
Fort Mohave, AZ

Rushmore Memorial Baseball Team jacket

My father, Orville Worman, was a Rushmore worker. I was raised with Mount Rushmore close by and hearing Rushmore stories whenever Nick Clifford, Merle Peterson, Howard Peterson, and other Rushmore workers visited us.

It is only after moving away from the Black Hills, and getting older, that I really appreciate what was accomplished. I continue to be amazed at what Mr. Borglum and his son Lincoln created with ordinary men and women as a workforce. It is truly a National Memorial and a Shrine of Democracy.

As a family, we continue to keep this great accomplishment alive in the memories of Orville's grandchildren and great-grandchildren.

Darrell Worman
Georgetown, TX

First-hand Account

At 97 years of age, I am so pleased to remember back when this wonderful legacy began. I feel I grew up with Rushmore, being only four when it all began. My family was there on that board platform when President Coolidge gave his dedication speech in 1927 and handed Borglum his drill tool to officially start the carving. I was also there at all four dedications, one for each presidential figure.

I remember John Boland who operated the Harvester implement store in Rapid City, held the Rushmore purse strings and was always a promoter. When I would go in the store with my dad or my uncle, the conversation always ended up being about Rushmore.

When I was a preteen, we lived 15 miles from Rushmore, and I would hear the noon and 4 pm dynamite blasting that took place when they were working on the mountain. The pheasants would crow their alarm a few seconds after each blast. I used to wait stark still during those few seconds, when every pheasant let the world know that a blast had occurred.

My cousin, George Hesnard, was one of the carvers. His sister Jo (who gave mine tours down in Keystone) worked with Mr. Borglum in publicizing the carving. There were a few times when Jo would take her mine tour group to the top of Rushmore, if it suited Borglum at the time. Jo was the first woman to be lowered in a bosun chair over Washington's nose. The Borglum women were the only others.

I also remember sitting in a college chemistry lecture when the news came over the radio that Gutzon Borglum had died. I will never forget that day in 1941.

As the years sailed by, I watched the dedication of the Memorial in 1991, fifty years after its completion in 1941. I became a charter member of the Mount Rushmore History Association Committee (of the Mount Rushmore Society) in 1993. We opened a bookstore at the park and previewed every book we carried. With the hundreds of times I've driven up to see Rushmore, I always have the same awesome feeling. I do not need a thing besides the faces to thrill me.

Geraldine Hesnard Evans
Mount Rushmore Society Member
Brighton, CO

Summer Love

After graduation from high school in May of 1969, I was accepted for summer employment at Mount Rushmore. It was a wonderful place to work and earn some additional money for college.

During the summer of 1969, I met this wonderful lady (Bev) who was working her second summer at Mount Rushmore. She worked in the Rushmore Dining Room as the head busgirl, and I worked in the stockroom.

On June 13 (Friday), we had six inches of snow fall on the grounds. In July, we were able to watch the moon landing as management hooked up TVs in the Dining Room so visitors and staff could watch history taking place. Bev and I were married in North Dakota in June 1972.

We return to the Black Hills as much as possible, particularly to the "Mountain," as the summer of 1969 was the beginning of a lifetime of wonderful, lasting memories. Our two sons have always said, "Thanks to Gutzon Borglum for Mount Rushmore," because we found each other there.

Bev and Bob Curtis
Rapid City, SD

The Seated Lincoln

In May 1989, with General and Mrs. Herbert Huber as our guests, our family ate in Mount Rushmore's Buffalo Café, looking out of the huge windows at the four presidential faces.

When our guests spied a statue outside one of the windows, they could not wait to see it up close and photograph it. They learned that this bronze statue had just been cast as a replica of Gutzon Borglum's "Seated Lincoln" in Newark, New Jersey.

The history of the original statue goes back to 1911 when the city of Newark commissioned Gutzon Borglum to cast a life-size bronze statue of Abraham Lincoln. This famous statue of Lincoln seated at one end of a bench with his top hat beside him was dedicated by President Theodore Roosevelt on Memorial Day, 1911. However, by 1986, the 75-year-old statue had become dilapidated from the effects of pollution and the corrosive pigeon droppings.

The Rushmore-Borglum Story Museum in Keystone, SD, came to the rescue. Representatives from the museum, including curator Howard Shaff, offered to restore the original bronze statue. However, the contract stipulated the museum be allowed to cast a replica after

the original had been restored. After legalities were ironed out, the original sculpture was shipped to a foundry in Bridgeport, CT. In three months, the replica was shipped back to Mount Rushmore.

The Buffalo Café and the other concessions had to be replaced during a facility renovation in the 1990s. Naturally, the replica of the "Seated Lincoln" needed a safe haven, so it was transported to the front of the Alex Johnson Hotel in Rapid City.

At the Alex Johnson Hotel, many tourists and locals took photos of loved ones sitting on the bench with President Lincoln. Watching all this interest, a businessman, Don Perdue, got an idea: "What if we had a whole downtown of presidents?" Thus, was born our downtown City of Presidents [in Rapid City].

Today, the "Seated Lincoln" replica welcomes all visitors to the Borglum-Rushmore Story Museum.

Eleanore Rowan Moe
Rapid City, SD

Patriots

We visited Mount Rushmore on the night of August 8, 2018. We started our day with a tour of the Badlands and were tired, but we decided to attend the Evening Lighting Ceremony at Mount Rushmore.

The ranger who made the presentation gave a wonderful overview of the four presidents on Mount Rushmore and the importance of each of them to the U.S. The program reminded us of patriotism, love of country and brought a tear to many eyes that evening.

The program concluded with the ranger inviting all veterans to come to the stage to be recognized. There was resounding applause for these living patriots. They carefully lowered the flag and lovingly folded it.

This presentation made us feel proud of our country and ever so glad that we had attended this program at Mount Rushmore on this night.

Georgia and David Dahnke
Bean Station, TN

Lakota Language

Never having seen Mount Rushmore in my 60+ years of life, I was thankful to be included in a road trip that was organized by my cousin.

On June 13, 2017, I rented Mount Rushmore Self-Guided Tours for everyone. They could choose from five different languages on these devices: English, Spanish, German, French, or Lakota.

As I walked through the Avenue of Flags that line the path to this famous monument, I listened to the tour in Lakota because I wanted to hear the sound of Native Americans from this region, even if I didn't understand it. It was like listening to music.

When I returned from my trek to the Sculptor's Studio, I saw a tipi and listened to Park Ranger Darrell Red Cloud's presentation. Red Cloud is the grandson of a Lakota chief who went to Washington D.C. to advocate for better housing, food and medical services for his people.

Red Cloud was an excellent storyteller with many materials we were able to feel and see. I learned so many interesting facts about how Gutzon Borglum (the sculptor) helped to convince local people to feed and clothe the Lakota tribe near the Black Hills.

Next, we went to the Gift Shop and saw Don "Nick" Clifford, the last surviving worker, then 96 years old. He autographed his book for my grandson. What a great opportunity to ask questions of him and his wife.

Thank you for the opportunity for me to tell my story about my Mount Rushmore experience.

Mrs. Leah Zenker
Levittown, PA

Epilogue

I was 12 years old when I first visited Mount Rushmore. It was August 1973, and my family was at the tail end of a three-week road trip, highlighted by nonstop car trouble, sibling rivalry, and a nervous dog.

By this point, my parents must have been desperate to get back home to Chicago. But instead of cutting the trip short, we drove to Mount Rushmore. And on that afternoon, we relaxed. All of us. Even the dog behaved.

Was it because of the watchful eyes of the presidents? Maybe. More likely, it was the sunshine, clear air, and the people.

Even now, I'm calmed, yet energized by watching people at Mount Rushmore: kids, families, couples, lone tourists, staff. Midst their interactions, I witness joy, unity, and peace.

Despite our country's recent challenges, the story of Mount Rushmore continues to be more than the carved faces. As I wrote in the first edition of *Mount Rushmore Memories*, the story of Mount Rushmore is the story of people.

On the facing page, write a few sentences about your memories of Mount Rushmore. When did you visit? Who were you with? What do you remember seeing, hearing, and feeling? And while you're at it, print one of your photos and paste it on the page.

You're part of Mount Rushmore's story.

Jean L.S. Patrick
Mitchell, SD
Mount Rushmore Author and
Memory Preservationist